The Authors

Maralene and Miles Wesner are multi-talented teachers and prolific writers. They have published more than 150 Audio-Visual Education aids, and pioneered new reading methods with their Phonics in a Nutshell (1965).

They have written articles, and mission studies for Southern Baptist periodicals. They were in the original group of writers to develop WMU's Big "A" Club material.

They've published several books with Broadman Press: *A Fresh Look at the Gospel* (1983); *You Are What You Choose* (1984); and *How To Be a Saint When You Feel Like a Sinner* (1986) and self-published 30 books by Diversity Press.

They are noted for their no-nonsense style, their clear illustrations, and their willingness to face controversial issues. From the dual perspectives of both academic and religious professions, they seek to be a bridge between the spiritual and the intellectual worlds.

They hold Masters Degrees (MEd) from Oklahoma University plus work toward a Doctorate. Miles also attended Southwestern Baptist Theological Seminary, and served as a high school counselor. He has been the bi-vocational pastor of a small rural church for more than 50 years.

Both Maralene and Miles taught in public school and collages and served as educational consultants. Maralene taught Psychology and Speech for Southeastern Oklahoma State University for 32 years. She was chosen Oklahoma Teacher of the Year in 1975.

They have planned, led tours, and done research in all of the 50 states, Canada, Mexico, Europe, Egypt, Japan, and the Holy Land. In 1985, they were among a small group of Americans who were invited by Dr. Joseph P. Kennedy of the US/China Education Foundation and Bishop Ting, leader of the Three Self Movement, to participate in the First Symposium on the Church in Nanjing, China.

Now, they use their lifetime of varied experiences to write insightful sermons, essays, and books.

Titles by Maralene & Miles Wesner
published by Nurturing Faith

Sermons for Special Days

Life More Abundant

Do You Really Know Jesus?

If Jesus Were Here Today

101 Sparks of Inspiration

When God Can't Answer

Think (Or Else!)

Stumbling to Zion

Sensible Sermons

Finding Truth in the Parables

The Unknown God

Maralene & Miles Wesner

Truth OR *Tradition?*

© 2024
Published in the United States by Nurturing Faith, Macon, GA.
Nurturing Faith is a book imprint of Good Faith Media (goodfaithmedia.org).
Library of Congress Cataloging-in-Publication Data is available.

ISBN: 978-1-63528-246-7

All rights reserved. Printed in the United States of America.

Scripture quotations are from New Revised Standard Version Bible Updated Edition, copyright © 2021 National Council of the Churches of Christ in the United States of America. Used by permission. All rights reserved worldwide.
Scripture quotations marked (KJV) are taken from the KING JAMES VERSION, public domain.

Cover photo by Debby Hudson on Unsplash.

Contents

Introduction 1

Section 1: Characteristics of the Gospel 9

Chapter 1: It's Profound, Not Trivial 11

Chapter 2: It's Positive, Not Negative 21

Chapter 3: It's Personalized, Not Standardized 31

Section 2: Principles of the Gospel 33

Chapter 4: God Is in Believers 41

Chapter 5: Power Is in Truth 51

Chapter 6: The Kingdom Is Among Us 61

Section 3: Purposes of the Gospel 71

Chapter 7: To Live It, Not Just Tell It 73

Chapter 8: To Enrich Lives, Not Just Win Souls 81

Chapter 9: To Share with Everyone, Not Just a Few 91

Conclusion 99

Introduction

In religious circles we are gospel-oriented. It's a constant theme. We're told to accept, share, and preach the gospel, yet few people even know what the gospel is!

In the New Testament the Greek word translated as *gospel* means to bring good tidings, to deliver a good message, or to announce good news. That's strange, because so much of what we commonly assume to be the gospel is not good news! The publication of the Ten Commandments is not especially good news; it contains a list of prohibitions. The warning of dire punishment is not good news. A tirade of threats, oughts, blames, and guilts is not good news. Being informed that you're a vile sinner is not good news. Being threatened with eternal punishment is not good news. Being told the world is evil is not good news.

So much tradition has gotten mixed in with truth that Christianity today is more often associated with bad news. Its leaders give critical discourses, and its members have judgmental attitudes.

Since Jesus initiated the idea of the gospel and since the word *gospel* defines and permeates his teachings, perhaps we need to discover what he meant by the term. Does the gospel mean a set of cut and dried answers? That's the gospel for many people!

A few years ago, a religious ad campaign featured one slogan: "Christ is the answer!" A group of confused teenagers approached their pastor and said, "Please, sir, we don't even know what the question is!" That's the problem with simplistic presentations. They make profound pronouncements about trivial, irrelevant things and leave the serious, life-changing issues untouched. Jesus knew that; therefore, he avoided absolute edicts and pat answers.

Does the gospel mean a list of strict rules that must be obeyed? That's the gospel for many people! Some church covenants and creeds are full of "do"s and "don't"s. Members anxiously ask, "What does the Bible say about this? What do our beliefs and doctrines say about that? Is this right? Is that wrong?" Since Jesus knew most decisions don't have clear and perfect yes-or-no resolutions, he avoided rigid rules.

Does the gospel present a brief formula that must be followed to achieve salvation? That's the gospel for many people! The first inquiries of troubled souls often ask, "What do I have to do to please God? What acts must I perform to get to heaven? What words do I have to say to be saved?" Since Jesus knew these methods are artificial and misleading, he refused to present empty formulas.

Strangely enough, it's what Jesus didn't say that's almost as significant as what he did say. What he omitted is so surprising and unexpected that we could almost label it the "unspoken gospel."

It's important to note that even though the prophets had predicted information about the gospel, they didn't truly understand it. There was a measure of validity in their message. They did grasp the hopeful nature of the messianic revelation, but their knowledge was incomplete.

The disciples proclaimed elements of the gospel, but they didn't fully understand it! There was a measure of validity in their message. They did grasp the fact that Jesus's emphasis on righteousness and concern for human welfare was beneficial, but their knowledge was incomplete.

It took Jesus himself to enunciate the gospel theme in its entirety. He was insightful enough to include the internal, psychological implications. He was able to go beneath the surface and deal with things like the alienation of guilt, the deceit of hypocrisy, the blessings of abundant life, and the importance of autonomy and productivity.

The gospel of Jesus differed radically from the repetitious dogmas of the past and the orthodox preoccupations of the priests. His gospel was simple and relevant. It was sanctified common sense! It cut straight through the mountains of legalistic beliefs and ritualistic customs that had accumulated over the centuries. It scoffed at the taboos and superstitions that were paralyzing ordinary people. It detested and repudiated the stranglehold that both the civil and religious authorities had on trusting peasants. Jesus's depth of understanding and discernment enabled him to separate truth from tradition.

The gospel of Jesus undid more than it did! It overrode the oppressive economic caste system by extending social benefits to the poor. It unlocked the emotional prisons of despair by offering hope to the broken hearted. It removed doctrinal chains and gave deliverance to the captive! It stripped away spiritual blindfolds and gave sight to the blind (see Luke 4:18–19)!

Only a divinely inspired gospel could liberate men and women from their irrational fears, obsessive guilt, and mindless conditioning. Only Jesus's gospel was good news! After listening to his enlightening and hopeful teachings, a few individuals began to believe that if God wasn't vindictive and ill-tempered, then perhaps religious ceremonies could be adapted to human needs. If there were no angry deities, demanding bribes and favors, then perhaps fasting and sacrifice were useful only insofar as they gave comfort to ordinary men and women.

The worth of every human being was Jesus's theme. The kingdom he envisioned and described promised a free and reasonable lifestyle. It was not tied to a deadly set of prescribed demands and appeasements. Eating without going through ritual ablutions wouldn't kill you! Failure to figure the exact number of seeds to donate wouldn't result in death. Walking one step too far on the Sabbath wouldn't lead to tragedy. This liberating and reassuring knowledge provided tremendous relief! This was good news!

The heavy burdens the Pharisees had been forcing upon the worshipers were finally lifted. Men and women didn't have to cower in fear if their food was mixed in an unorthodox way or cringe in terror if the blood of the sacrifice was incorrectly applied. We can't imagine the misery experienced by these unsophisticated people. They sincerely believed a powerful being was waiting to punish anyone who deviated from proper procedures or failed to obey every trivial rule.

Amid these oppressive conditions Jesus's gospel was definitely good news to those who lived with anxiety and guilt. His yoke was truly light in comparison to that of the scribes and Pharisees. Contrary to popular opinion, the gospel didn't tell people what they had to do. Instead, it told them what they didn't have to do! The gospel didn't add more rules.

Instead, it revoked many of the current rules. The gospel didn't present new formulas and rituals for salvation. Instead, it discarded many of the time-honored formulas and rituals that had been carefully preserved for centuries.

In analyzing Jesus's gospel we see that it had three main characteristics: First, it gave general profound guidelines instead of specific trivial requirements. Second, it suggested positive initiatives instead of imposing negative prohibitions. Third, it offered personalized recommendations that could be adjusted in a changing world instead of setting absolute standardized mandates.

Of course, not everyone agreed with these more progressive doctrines and this more relaxed lifestyle. Many Pharisees and priests accused Jesus of destroying religion. This always happens when spiritual seekers attempt to change, improve, or update traditional religious beliefs and practices. It's surprising that humanity tends to put up self-constructed barriers and inhabit self-made prisons. A policeman tells of a family whose members literally caused their own deaths. They had a paranoid fear of criminals and therefore fortified their home with such effective barricades that when a fire broke out, no one could escape.

Many orthodox Jews of Jesus's day had done that. Their self-constructed barriers were limiting their growth. Their self-made prisons were stifling progress. They had religious rules and regulations for every possible situation. Their doctrines dictated every detail of life. Jesus abolished such barriers and unlocked such prisons.

In analyzing Jesus's gospel we see that it was also based on three main principles: First, it described God as a spirit within the hearts of believers instead of as a physical deity out there in some holy place. Second, it insisted upon gaining credibility and power through the discovery of truth instead of depending upon the efficacy of authority and tradition. Third, it depicted the kingdom as being a state of mind and a way of life that provides abundant joys and rewards now instead of being just a future utopian paradise.

Religion is often misunderstood because people tend to concoct elaborate ideologies, which are susceptible to superstition. Valuable insights and practical instructions can quickly degenerate into distorted notions. During an epidemic in a primitive country, a well-meaning doctor noticed that the natives all drank from a common dipper. He explained that if they would always use a sanitary drinking cup, then that would prevent the disease from spreading. After an absence of several weeks, he returned to find even worse conditions and even more illness. He reprimanded the village chief for not following his instructions. "Oh, but we did, Doctor," the old man replied. "We bought a sanitary cup just like you said, and we're making everybody use it!" It's obvious that blind obedience without understanding can be useless and even disastrous.

Likewise, blind obedience to religious precepts without an adequate understanding of the reasons behind them can become not only useless, but actually destructive.

In analyzing Jesus's gospel, we see that it also had three main purposes: First, it emphasized that we should be showing people what to do instead of just telling them what to do. Second, it emphasized that we should be improving and enriching people's physical, mental, and spiritual lives instead of just winning disembodied souls. Third, it emphasized the importance of sharing the good news with everyone instead of neglecting the lost and the least.

Some people tend to be fearful and selfish when it comes to sharing. This selfishness is based upon a mistaken idea that giving to you will diminish me. Now, some things are finite. If you have five apples and give two away, you will have fewer for yourself. Other things, however, are infinite. We can give knowledge, love, and spiritual truth to others without diminishing our own supply. In fact, giving those things away actually increases our own supply!

Following a tornado, many families were being temporarily housed in a large armory. Since there was a power outage, some of the groups used lamps or candles to illuminate their living space. Nearby households, without such devices, lived by their neighbors' light. Now, the ones with the lamps didn't have less light because others were also benefiting. If they had put their flames "under bushel baskets" or hidden them with shades, in a selfish attempt to hoard their light and deprive their neighbors, they would have had less for themselves. Sharing and cooperating can be mutually beneficial.

It's hard to believe, but a gospel that advocates autonomy and liberty is not popular with everyone. Many people want authorities to tell them what to do so they don't have to think for themselves. They want things spelled out in black and white so they don't have to make difficult decisions. They want to be dependent to avoid blame if something goes wrong. Such attitudes are incompatible with life in a kingdom of mature individuals.

Some people deny reality because they want their favorite illusions to remain intact. They want their comfortable beliefs to be unquestioned. They want their cherished fantasies to remain undisturbed. Such attitudes are incompatible with life in a kingdom of responsible individuals.

Then, quite a few people want to protect their beliefs by isolating them. They are disturbed when opposing views are expressed. They are frightened when other perspectives are revealed. They want to keep their faith system locked up in a safety deposit box, untouched by examination or controversy. Such attitudes are incompatible with life in a kingdom of productive individuals.

Maturity, responsibility, and productivity require both logical thinking and physical effort. That's why the gospel is not good news to everyone. Even when Jesus was ministering in person, his message was utterly rejected by the vast majority of the population. Those who were shallow-minded, fearful, and materialistic all saw it as a threat!

The same thing is true today. There are those who seem to believe God wants us to be puppets or robots. They say we should be totally dependent and totally submissive. They claim we must let God dictate our words and determine our moves. Their popular motto expresses it this way: "Let go, and let God."

That's not what the gospel teaches. God never tells us to "let go" or "give up." Instead, he calls us to autonomy and self-direction. It's immature human beings, not God, who resist the gift of freedom. These people don't want to face hard choices. They want life neatly laid out with all routes clearly marked and all uncertainties clearly resolved. This arrangement might be pleasant, but it would be counterproductive. Struggle is essential for growth. Energetic movement is part of God's overall plan. Change is desirable. Jesus advocated "new wine in new bottles"!

Apathy and inertia are not productive. If you step on a descending escalator, you don't have to deliberately walk down to go down. In fact, you have to move steadily upward to counteract the regressive movement. The same thing is true of gravity in the physical world and inaction in the spiritual world. You don't have to deliberately move downward to go down. If you just stand still, you'll be pulled down. You have to move steadily upward to maintain your position.

We haven't done that in theological areas. Progress in religious thought is stymied today. Development in theology has stood still for over two thousand years. That's tragic! We must deepen our understanding and broaden our vision to carry out Jesus's ministry in the twenty-first century.

So what is the gospel? It's not pat answers. It's not rigid rules. It's not empty formulas. The gospel is the good news that God is a loving spirit in us, rather than a powerful creature out there. The gospel is the good news that power is dependent upon the discovery and practice of truth, rather than the performance of rituals and obedience to authority. The gospel is the good news that the kingdom is something to be enjoyed in this present world, rather than something to be hoped for in a future world.

The gospel does require commitment. The attributes of caring, sharing, and daring must permeate our lifestyle if we're to make a difference. The gospel is good news for you if you're the kind of person who wants to worship a God of spirit and truth. It's good news for you if you want to experience reality and live life to the fullest. It's good news for you if you want to be free and independent. It's good news for you if you want to think and grow. It's good news for you if you want to be productive and creative in helping to develop a better world.

Once, a group of tech enthusiasts combined current data with historical information and ran the material through a computer. The machine came up with this alarming conclusion—if our civilization is obliterated, it will not be by an Armageddon battle or a nuclear bomb, but by these three malicious ideas: If we begin to believe we are not morally responsible for our own conduct, we'll cease to exist. If we begin to believe we are not economically responsible for our own welfare, we'll cease to exist. If we begin to believe we are not politically responsible for our own government, we'll cease to exist. Those are valid predictions!

As Christians we must not espouse any theology that undermines such self-determination. We must not teach a defective and deadly ideology of submission and irresponsibility. We must not propagate any doctrine that encourages personal apathy. The gospel of Jesus calls us to action and maturity! To understand and obey this gospel, we must learn how to separate truth from tradition.

Section 1

Characteristics of the Gospel

Chapter 1

It's Profound, Not Trivial

"You...have neglected the weightier matters of the law: justice and mercy and faith." (Matt 23:23)

A bewildered student faced this assignment: "Describe the meaning of life in ten words or less." We all want such definite information, and we want it now! We all want our dilemmas resolved perfectly and immediately. We all want a reliable answering machine at our disposal. Many people expect religion to fill this need. They want to pop in a prayer and get out a miracle. They use the Bible as if it were a divine fortune cookie. They view God as a holy drill sergeant who gives strict orders and metes out punishment.

If we examine Jesus's style and ministry, however, the first characteristic we notice is that he avoided easy answers. He dealt with general profound values, not with specific trivial details. He was hard to pin down and at times downright exasperating.

Once, Jesus was confronted with this seemingly simple question: "Who is my mother?" You'd think he would have quickly responded. Surely this inquiry had only one specific answer. But even here he was not direct. He immediately moved to another level by asking, "'Who is my mother, and who are my brothers?' And pointing to his disciples, he said, 'Here are my mother and my brothers! For whoever does the will of my Father in heaven is my brother and sister and mother'" (Matt 12:48–50).

Jesus often gave ambiguous, thought-provoking replies to questions. When the Jews asked, "How long will you keep us in suspense? If you are the Messiah, tell us plainly," Jesus replied, "I told you, and you do not believe. The works that I do in my Father's name testify to me" (John 10:24–25). He was encouraging them to observe, analyze, and draw their own conclusions.

Sometimes he suggested theoretically possible but seemingly impractical solutions to social problems. When Peter asked, "Lord, if my brother or sister sins against me, how often should I forgive? As many as seven times?" Jesus answered, "Not seven times, but, I tell you, seventy-seven times" (Matt 18:21–22). Now, individuals could probably get such a count if they kept a list of every insignificant disagreement. But since no one can remember that many incidents, Jesus was really saying, "Don't try to keep a legal count; just be a forgiving person!"

If inquiries about ethics or doctrine were made, he invariably countered with another question. When John the Baptist's disciples came asking, "Why do we and the Pharisees fast often, but your disciples do not fast?" Jesus answered, "The wedding attendants cannot mourn as long as the bridegroom is with them, can they?" (Matt 9:14–15).

One day "Pharisees and scribes came to Jesus from Jerusalem and said, 'Why do your disciples break the tradition of the elders? For they do not wash their hands before they eat.'" Jesus replied, "And why do you break the commandment of God for the sake of your tradition?" (Matt 15:1–3).

Another time "someone came to him and said, 'Teacher, what good deed must I do to have eternal life?' And he said to him, 'Why do you ask me about what is good? There is one who is good. If you wish to enter into life, keep the commandments" (Matt 19:16–17).

In each of these examples Jesus avoided specific answers and instead urged people to consider the deeper implications. This habitual method of response confused his disciples and infuriated the Pharisees. Many people dislike having their minds challenged or their beliefs questioned. They don't want to think, and they certainly don't want to deal with intellectual confrontations. That's why the religious leaders became so insecure and frustrated in the face of Jesus's brilliant scrutiny that they retreated. The scripture says, "No one was able to give him an answer, nor from that day did anyone dare to ask him any more questions" (Matt 22:46).

When people urged him to make moral decisions for them, he usually responded with a story, a parable, or an analogy. Once, "The disciples came to Jesus and asked, 'Who is greatest in the kingdom of heaven?' He called a child, whom he put among them, and said, 'Truly I tell you, unless you change and become like children, you will never enter the kingdom of heaven'" (Matt 18:1–3).

Jesus seemed to have a story for everything. Even his disciples complained about this, saying, "Why do you speak to them in parables?" (Matt 13:10). He used nondirective counseling techniques long before there were any professional psychologists. He encouraged people to think for themselves. He knew that understanding and wisdom can't be given to a person. As students we can't be told; we have to discover! We can't be taught; we have to learn!

When a hostile group tried to trick him with a politically loaded question, he responded with a simple verifiable question: "'Is it lawful to pay taxes to Caesar or not?' But Jesus, aware of their malice, said, 'Why are you putting me to the test, you hypocrites? Show me the coin used for the tax.' And they brought him a denarius. Then he said to them, 'Whose head is this and whose title?' They answered, 'Caesar's.' Then he said to them, 'Give therefore to Caesar the things that are Caesar's and to God the things that are God's'" (Matt 22:16–21).

When the chief priests and the elders of the people brought up a hot issue, saying,

> "By what authority are you doing these things, and who gave you this authority?" Jesus said to them, "I will ask you one thing question; if you tell me the answer, then I will also tell you by what authority I do these things. Did the baptism of John come from heaven, or was it of human origin?" And they argued with one another, "If we say, 'From heaven,' he will say to us, 'Why, then, did you not believe him?' But if we say, 'Of human origin,' we are afraid of the crowd, for all regard John as a prophet." So they answered Jesus, "We do not know."

> And he said to them, "Neither will I tell you by what authority I am doing these things." (Matt 21:23–27)

When another group alluded to a popular theological controversy about marriage and the resurrection, he pointed them to a deeper level:

> The same day some Sadducees came to him saying there is no resurrection, and they asked him a question: "Teacher, Moses said, 'If a man dies childless, his brother shall marry the widow and raise up children for his brother.' Now there were seven brothers among us; the first married and died childless, leaving the widow to his brother. The second did the same, so also the third, down to the seventh. Last of all, the woman herself died. In the resurrection, then, whose wife of the seven will she be? For all of them had married her." Jesus answered them, "You are wrong because you know neither the scriptures nor the power of God. For in the resurrection people neither marry nor are given in marriage but are like angels of God in heaven. (Matt 22:23–30)

When a group quoted Moses's commandment concerning the penalty for adultery, his response was astute. He didn't criticize the Old Testament rule or argue about the justice of the punishment. Instead, he made it personal:

> The scribes and the Pharisees brought a woman who had been caught in adultery, and, making her stand before all of them, they said to him, "Teacher, this woman was caught in the very act of committing adultery. Now in the law Moses commanded us to stone such women. Now what do you say?" They said this to test him, so that they might have some charge to bring against him. Jesus bent down and wrote with his finger on the ground. When they kept on questioning him, he straightened up and said to them, "Let anyone among you who is

without sin be the first to throw a stone at her." (John 8:3–7).

When individuals asked for special favors, he explained that such things were out of his hands:

> Then the mother of the sons of Zebedee came to him with her sons, and kneeling before him, she asked a favor of him.... She said to him, "Declare that these two sons of mine will sit, one at your right hand and one at your left, in your kingdom." But Jesus answered, "You do not know what you are asking. Are you able to drink the cup that I am about to drink?" They said to him, "We are able." He said to them, "You will indeed drink my cup, but to sit at my right hand and at my left, this is not mine to grant, but it is for those for whom it has been prepared by my Father." (Matt 20:20–23)

If there are specific, concrete answers to complex religious and ethical questions, why didn't he give them? If one word or phrase could resolve a conflict, why didn't he simply say it and avoid all the confusion? If spiritual truths can be expressed in perfect, infallible, right-or-wrong terms, why were his explanations so ambiguous?

Some of his statements can lend themselves to outright misinterpretations if taken literally. For instance, he said, "For the Son of Man is to come with his angels in the glory of his Father, and then he will repay everyone for what has been done. Truly I tell you, there are some standing here who will not taste death before they see the Son of Man coming in his kingdom" (Matt 16:27–28). Of course, we know he did not set up a visible kingdom, complete with angels and rewards within that generation, even though his words seem to justify that interpretation.

He also said, "Truly I tell you, there is no one who has left house or brothers or sisters or mother or father or children or fields for my sake and for the sake of the good news who will not receive a hundredfold now in this age—houses, brothers and sisters, mothers and children, and fields, with persecutions—and in the age to come eternal life"

(Mark 10:29–30). But his disciples did not receive other family members or possessions, as his statements seem to promise.

It's evident that many of his words have been misunderstood. Some were not literal. For instance, he said, "Destroy this temple, and in three days I will raise it up" (John 2:19). He was not actually planning to rebuild the temple in three days; rather, he was referring to his resurrection. He also said, "Everyone who lives and believes in me will never die" (John 11:26). Those who believed in him did not live forever in the physical sense, as that scripture seems to suggest; rather, he was referring to eternal life.

Many of his observations have led to false doctrines when taken out of context. For instance, he said, "They will pick up snakes, and if they drink any deadly thing, it will not hurt them" (Mark 16:18). However, believers are not miraculously protected from venomous snakes and poisonous drinks, as this passage seems to indicate. Modern readers don't understand that the words *serpents* and *poison* were local idiomatic expressions for evil.

If Jesus knew what was best and used the most effective approach, then we must assume life's problems require general, open-ended explanations and that trying to supply simple, definite answers or impose quick, shallow solutions is counterproductive. Rather, individuals must be enabled to create their own satisfactory answers and develop their own permanent solutions.

It's obvious that great insights and great ideas can only be transferred as seeds! Even in horticulture, full-grown specimens can't be transplanted without damage. It's more profitable to plant an acorn than it is to dig up and try to reset a giant oak tree. The same thing is true in other areas. It's easier to plant a thought than it is to indoctrinate groups with an entire system of theology. It's more efficient to instill an aspiration than it is to impose an entire value system.

We all face situations that force us to decide whether to tell people something or to help them discover it for themselves. In Jesus's interviews and encounters he never said, "This is the right answer to that question!" or "This is the correct solution to that problem!" Such a response is not helpful. When the next question or the next problem arises, the person will be just as confused as ever. To achieve permanent stability individuals must develop their own techniques for finding valid answers to questions and finding logical solutions to problems.

For instance, if a child needs to know the sum of four plus three plus two, you can either tell him it is nine or show him how to do the mathematical process called addition. If you merely tell him the answer is nine, his immediate need will be satisfied. But when he meets four plus three plus one, he will be stymied again. If you teach him how to add, however, then the solution to all future problems of this nature will be within his grasp.

By dealing with trivial questions and problems, you are wasting your time. By providing specific answers and solutions to these questions and problems, you are keeping individuals dependent and immature. On the other hand, by providing general instruction you are making them independent and mature. Contrary to what some people think, Jesus did not want to keep his followers dependent upon him. He encouraged them to be autonomous, saying, "You will know the truth, and the truth will make you free" (John 8:32).

Many political, social, and religious demagogues have noted that giving cut-and-dried answers will make you popular. It will impress your audience and assure you of gaining numerous adoring fans. That's probably true, but it won't accomplish long-term goals or develop a responsible constituency. Dictatorial leaders may gain temporary fame, but they will lose permanent respect. The false prophets had the answer, and the people rallied. Hitler had the answer, and the people rallied. Gurus like Jim Jones had the answer, and the people rallied. In each case, however, their moment of glory was short-lived. Their success ultimately turned to ashes. They left their followers and the world worse off with a sorry legacy.

It's regrettable that these lessons from history have not changed public opinion. Even today, thoughtful politicians, ministers, and educators who prefer to deal with broader issues and discuss more profound implications are often criticized for being indecisive, whereas those who respond to all inquiries with glib certainties are applauded. Under these circumstances it's tempting to declare "yes" or "no" without hesitation. It's tempting to label everything in unequivocal terms of right or wrong. It's tempting to give an answer even when you don't have one!

Fortunately, Jesus overcame this temptation. He's to be commended for avoiding the specific facts and emphasizing the deeper meanings. Specific facts are only useful to one person in one situation at one time, while general information about the issues can be applied by all people in all areas of life at any time!

Specific facts tend to produce distorted tangents while general explanations give a sensible, balanced overview. Specific facts change while general principles endure in all ages and all cultures. A citizen of this fast-changing society expressed it well when he complained, "Just about the time I find the answers, they change the questions." This is an ever-present problem.

Becoming distracted by current conditions is a common failure of moral reformers. Picking out one specific evil to attack seems to be an exercise in futility. Each generation has its sin fad.

Puritans deplored less than ankle-length skirts. Billy Sunday castigated men for wearing ruffled shirts and women for chewing gum. In the more recent past evangelists have condemned liquor and dancing. Today it's drugs and pornography. Such preoccupation with overt particulars is not a new phenomenon.

Both individuals and crowds were constantly demanding that Jesus turn his attention to specific local problems. He refused, and that's why his gospel is timeless! If he had spent his days planning crusades against licentious Roman baths and organizing protests against the Sadducees' heresy concerning immortality, we'd have a Bible full of useless, obsolete rules and regulations instead of a living gospel. The general admonition, "Do unto others as you'd have others do unto you," is valid for any age. The specific command, "Thou shalt not give tribute money to Caesar," is not! That's why Jesus refused to deal with specific issues (see Luke 20:22–25).

In fact, Jesus's method of handling personal moral decisions was very different from many preachers and pious church leaders today. He never gave advice about superficial things. He never criticized people's dress or food and drink or recreation. He never told people what activities to avoid or what hairstyles to choose. He left such matters up to each individual.

We can become so enamored with enticing tangents that we forget the essential and irreducible core. Once, an experienced crew of well-trained pilots became so involved in trying to find and replace a nonessential light bulb that they crashed the plane and killed many passengers. Distractions can be deadly!

Specific answers may be comforting, but specific answers do not promote mature and responsible behavior. Specific answers may make life easier, but specific answers do not encourage creative thought. Specific answers may help me today, but specific answers will not be universally applicable. Those leaders who major in specific answers to trivial questions develop passive followers and achieve transient fame. Those who major in general instructions about profound questions develop active disciples and make permanent contributions.

Jesus didn't want to attract passive, irresponsible followers. He wanted to develop active, intelligent disciples who ultimately would be able to make the kingdom he envisioned a reality. He explained this, saying, "If you continue in my word, you are truly my disciples" (John 8:31). In other words, talk is cheap! Voicing agreement is easy; incorporating that belief system into an everyday lifestyle is much harder but more productive.

By analyzing Jesus's gospel we've learned that his teachings dealt with profound general issues rather than trivial specific details. He was able to emphasize this important characteristic by separating truth from tradition.

Chapter 2

It's Positive, Not Negative

"Overcome evil with good." (Rom 12:21)

Many teenagers hear this litany before a date: "Don't text and drive! Don't hang out with the wrong crowd! Don't stay out too late. But have a good time, honey!"

Parents and authority figures often feel obligated to give well-defined lists of prohibitions. Legal systems have been predicated upon lists of prohibitions. Religious institutions have been organized around lists of prohibitions. We love our rules and regulations.

Surprisingly, when we examine Jesus's style and teaching, the second characteristic we notice is that he avoided lists of prohibitions. He even shortened the Ten Commandments to two positive statements: "Love God, and love people" (see Matt 22:37–39). He didn't give hard and fast rules, and he always dealt with the positive, not the negative!

In both his message and his ministry, there was a strange absence of condemnation. He didn't go on moral crusades. He didn't stress any particular flaws, faults, and failures. There were very few "thou shalt nots" in his vocabulary! He wasn't against sin as much as he was *for* people. When a person approached him for help, he never asked for confessions of past transgressions. He never demanded apologies for shortcomings. He never required repentance for misdeeds. When the impotent man by the pool needed assistance, he didn't say, "Admit your unworthiness, say you're sorry for what you've done, express proper remorse, and I'll consider your plight." Instead, he said, "Go and sin no more" (see John 5:1–15).

Jesus ignored the past and emphasized the future. He was not as much concerned with what we have been as he was with what we will be. He didn't deal as much with what we have done as he did with what we will do! When a person approached him for help, Jesus seldom made formal demands for allegiance. When blind Bartimaeus cried for mercy, he didn't say, "Bartimaeus, will you believe in me and follow me from now on?" He didn't say, "How loyal will you be? How faithful will you be?" Instead, he said, "What do you want me to do for you?" (see Mark 10:45–52). As soon as this man asked for sight, it was given with no strings attached.

When people approached him for help, Jesus never made them promise to reform. When the man with palsy was let down through the roof, he didn't say, "Will you solemnly swear to forsake your evil ways? Will you shape up and be a credit to my movement?" Instead, he said, "You're forgiven and healed. Get up and go home" (see Mark 2:3–11).

To those who think Christians should be separated from the world, he seems quite compromising. To those who think Christians should stand unequivocally against sin, he seems quite permissive. To those who think believers should shun every appearance of evil, he seems quite careless. He fraternized with pagans. He ate with sinners. He conversed with lawbreakers. He associated with prostitutes. He complimented heathens. In short, his lifestyle seems extraordinarily lax regarding pure standards.

When a woman was literally caught in the act of sexual immorality, he didn't punish her, criticize her, or shame her. To some moralists, the casual remark that she should "sin no more" seems considerably less than adequate (see John 8:11).

When the thief on the cross, requested clemency, Jesus didn't reprimand him for his life of crime. Instead, he calmly assured him, "Today you will be with me in paradise" (Luke 23:43).

In the story of the prodigal son, this delinquent, who broke every rule in the book, didn't make any amends or voice any resolutions, yet he was forgiven and rewarded (see Luke 15).

It's startling to realize that this same rebellious son would probably have been stoned to death if these parents had followed Old Testament requirements. According to the scriptures, God had commanded a strict penalty for the behavior of such a youth:

> If someone has a stubborn and rebellious son who will not obey his father and mother, who does not heed them when they discipline him, then his father and his mother shall take hold of him and bring him out to the elders of his town at the gate of that place. They shall say to the elders of his town, "This son of ours is stubborn and rebellious. He will not obey us. He is a glutton and a drunkard." Then all the men of the town shall stone him to death." (Deut 21:18–21)

Jesus didn't mention Moses's law or any punishment. Instead, he spoke of hugs and new clothes and celebrations. Evidence suggests Jesus was soft on sin! One of his most startling statements was made to a group of chief priests and elders: "Truly I tell you, the tax collectors and the prostitutes are going into the kingdom of God ahead of you" (Matt 21:31). He didn't even stipulate that those thieves and harlots he was describing were those who had been "converted and rehabilitated"!

These tax collectors and prostitutes included deceitful traitors and immoral women. The group of chief priests and elders included religious leaders who obeyed every rule and kept every commandment. This was an astonishing comparison. Surely these devout individuals were better than those sinners and thieves in the other group. These upright citizens worshiped regularly in the synagogues. They memorized scripture and wore those scriptures in little boxes on their foreheads. They tithed all their income, even the tiny spice seeds. They kept the law so perfectly that they wouldn't eat an egg that had been laid on the Sabbath, and they counted every step they took on that holy day.

Nevertheless, Jesus realized that although sexual promiscuity and stealing were wrong, he knew that such sinners are more likely to repent than the pious individuals who denied and excused all their faults. Furthermore, the sins of the publicans and prostitutes didn't do as much long-term psychological damage to society as the judgmental attitudes and critical tongues of the self-righteous hypocrites.

Of course, Jesus's radical remarks could encourage immorality. Such a cavalier attitude toward conventional propriety could undermine authority. Such a lack of emphasis on virtue could be construed as a license to sin! If it were anyone other than Jesus, we'd reprimand them for condoning wrongdoing!

If right is right and wrong is wrong, then why on earth didn't Jesus tell us which is which? If ethics aren't situational, if morals are truly unchanging, then why didn't he clearly enumerate the "do"s and "don't"s? If behavior standards can really be expressed in infallible terms, then why didn't he spend a little time spelling it out? Just a short document on rules and regulations would have prevented so much destructive wrangling. Innumerable splits have occurred; controversies have arisen; disagreements have persisted. Sincere, dedicated people agonize over crucial either/or decisions. Great suffering and irreparable harm result from honest mistakes. Surely if it were possible to establish absolute guidelines, Jesus would have done so!

Many people live in a rigid world. They see everybody and everything as either totally right or totally wrong. They have a good/bad mentality, but life isn't like that. We can't always respond to simple questions with a yes or no answer. For instance, is it right to throw a baby from a second-story window? One man got a medal for doing that, and another man went to prison for doing that. You see, the situations and motives were different. One did it from a burning building to firemen below, and the other did it because he was angry with the baby's mother.

Trying to fit all decisions into watertight compartments is a dangerous habit. Religion becomes one box, business another, family another, and recreation another. This forces people to operate in certain areas without the moral restraints that are present in other areas. Good church members can be fraudulent businessmen, and terrorists can be devoted to their faith and yet be vicious with enemies. Remember, there are a lot of color shades besides black and white. Many choices must be between "good and better" and "bad and worse." Mature people learn how to live with compromise, tolerance, and ambivalence. Jesus did! One day he couldn't even label Peter as being either good or bad. When he asked,

> "But who do you say that I am?" Simon Peter answered, "You are the Messiah, the Son of the living God." And Jesus answered him, "Blessed are you, Simon son of Jonah! For flesh and blood has not revealed this to you but my Father in heaven. And I tell you, you are Peter, and on this rock I will build my church, and the gates of Hades will not prevail against it. I will give you the keys of the kingdom of heaven, and whatever you bind on earth will be bound in heaven, and whatever you loose on earth will be loosed in heaven." (Matt 16:15–19)

Yet a short time later he said to this same Peter, "Get behind me, Satan! You are a hindrance to me" (Matt 16:23).

Since Jesus knew what was best and used the most effective approach, we must assume that setting up a predetermined moral code is not possible. We must assume that giving a list of prohibitions is not feasible. We must assume that making a list of rules is a waste of time. He knew that a positive approach is the most constructive and that acceptance and affirmation will eventually make negative criticism and condemnation unnecessary.

We know that trying to break a bad habit is extremely difficult. Concentrating on simply eliminating an objectionable practice is an exercise in futility. It's much more profitable to replace an undesirable habit with a desirable one. Jesus illustrated this principle with a story about seven demons:

> When the unclean spirit has gone out of a person, it wanders through waterless regions looking for a resting place, but it finds none. Then it says, "I will return to my house from which I came." When it returns, it finds it empty, swept, and put in order. Then it goes and brings along seven other spirits more evil than itself, and they enter and live there, and the last state of that person is worse than the first. (Matt 12:43–45)

This parable reveals the depth of Jesus's psychological insights. He knew what was in man. He knew it is the nature of human beings to abhor a vacuum. Men and women must hold certain values, believe certain precepts, and carry out certain activities. If no good ones are available, then they will settle for bad ones. This is true in the physical realm. If people are hungry, they will eat junk food, garbage, or whatever they can get. All the warnings, denunciations, and criticisms in the world will accomplish nothing. Since the void in their stomachs must be filled with something, you are much more likely to achieve your aim by providing good nutritional substitutes than by just forbidding the junk food.

The same thing is true in the spiritual realm. If people are bored, with nothing to do, they will turn to pornography, alcohol, drugs, or whatever destructive type of recreation they can find. All the warnings, denunciations, and criticisms in the world will accomplish nothing. You are much more likely to achieve your aim by providing challenging activities than by forbidding the obscene ones. In fact, moralists can increase the influence of evil when they ban certain books and forbid certain movies. This gives them notoriety and makes them more attractive. That's why Jesus said, "Ignore the tares." Don't waste your time denouncing the bad; magnify the good!

Once, a young man went off to college. After a few weeks his mother visited the campus and inspected his room in the dorm. To her dismay she found that one wall was covered with lewd photographs. The mother could have ordered this tasteless and embarrassing material removed. She could have expressed her disapproval. She could have shamed the boy or threatened him with reprisal. She could have, but she didn't.

Instead, she said nothing. After returning home she bought a large, expensive print of Sallman's classic painting *Head of Christ*. She put it in a beautiful frame and mailed it to her son. The enclosed note said, "Please hang this gift in your room."

The next time she visited the dorm, the new painting was displayed in a prominent place, and the pornographic material had been removed. A wise mother knew you must replace the negative with the positive. She didn't denounce the bad; she magnified the good!

Jesus also magnified the good. He praised the concern of the good Samaritan. He complimented the faith of the Roman centurion. He even rewarded the clever retort of the Syrophoenician woman.

When Jesus met Zacchaeus, he could have said, "Now look here, you rascal, you must not go around cheating people. You must not be so greedy! You must not hoard money!" He could have, but he didn't.

Instead, he said nothing of a negative nature, but rather offered to visit with him. The friendly overture sent this message: "You are a worthy person. I want to meet you and get to know you, so I'm going home with you." He didn't denounce the bad; he magnified the good. As a result Zacchaeus freely volunteered to do much more than would have been expected. He expressed an astonishingly liberal attitude. He went the second and third mile without any type of coercion. Acceptance and affirmation made criticism and condemnation unnecessary (see Luke 19:2–9).

When the prostitute brought the alabaster box full of ointment, Jesus could have said, "Now, wait just a minute. You have some serious problems. There are things in your background we need to discuss. I can't overlook immorality. Have you repented and renounced your past? Have you made a public confession of your sins? Do you vow to forsake that lifestyle in the future?" He could have, but he didn't.

Instead, he said nothing of a negative nature, but rather graciously accepted her gift. He praised her motives, defended her to her critics, and held her up as a model forever. He didn't denounce the bad; he magnified the good. Jesus knew that his accepting attitude would lead to great loyalty, so he explained, "He who is forgiven much loves much" (see Luke 7:47).

When the woman of Samaria confronted Jesus, he could have said, "Lady, you've really blown it. Your life's a mess! Five husbands—that's revolting! Flouting your disregard for social customs by living openly with a lover—that's disgusting! You dare to stand here questioning my theology? Why, you're not fit to worship in mountains or temples! Repent and move out of your present den of iniquity, and then I might be willing to talk to you!" He could have, but he didn't!

Instead, he said nothing of a negative nature, but rather treated her with respect. He didn't force her to espouse his own traditions. He didn't lecture her on proper morals. In short, he didn't denounce the bad; he magnified the good. In her gratitude she became his most enthusiastic admirer and influenced an entire city (see John 4:4–42).

It's unfortunate that when modern Christians advocate the same kind of positive acceptance exemplified by Jesus, they are severely criticized. Those who stress human possibilities are often accused of failing to deal with the "sin question." Those who offer unqualified forgiveness are charged with advocating a dangerous attitude of permissiveness. Those who constantly look for the best in their associates are ridiculed as being naive and unrealistic.

What motivates these reactions? Since we know we're supposed to follow Jesus's example and conform to his teachings, why don't we do it? Obviously it's because we don't have the same faith in people and the same devotion to truth that Jesus did. It's because we have a greater need to censure, retaliate, and punish than Jesus did. It's because we don't believe grace really works! Most of us give lip service to religious principles, but we prefer to emphasize the "don't"s rather than the "do"s. Most of us give lip service to religious practices, but we are more proficient in the judging areas than in the forgiving areas. We notice the one dirty spot on a garment and disregard all the clean parts.

These negative attitudes prove that we don't really believe the gospel! Jesus's teachings embody valid psychological principles. He realized that guilt is only useful when it motivates us to change. He realized that egotism is synonymous with inferiority. People who constantly boast about their purity and dedication don't really believe it. Instead, they are merely trying to cover up the terrible fear that they are worthless!

We all feel weak, unworthy, and ashamed of our inadequacies. We don't need constant reminders of our shortcomings. Instead, we need reassurance that we have strengths as well as weaknesses, abilities as well as limitations, and faith as well as doubts. We especially need reassurance that our failures aren't final.

It's significant that after Peter's shameful denials Jesus offered no reprimands and asked for no apologies. Instead, he gave him an important mission, saying, "Feed my sheep."

Criticism and condemnation set up a vicious cycle. They increase our feelings of guilt, which in turn increases our tendency to engage in defensive actions. Our self-preservation instinct causes us to mount counterattacks whenever we feel threatened. Under these circumstances no good is ever achieved.

In the fable of the wind and the sun, these two forces argued as to who was stronger. They agreed that the one who could make a man remove his coat would be declared superior. The wind tried with cold blasts, but the man held his coat tighter than ever. It tried with fierce gales, but the man clutched his coat more firmly than ever. The sun used no such methods. It merely shined. In its friendly, comfortable presence, the man relaxed. He no longer felt threatened. As soon as he became confident and warm, he voluntarily removed his coat. This proves that love is stronger than hate and honey is better than vinegar in attracting people as well as in catching flies.

A missionary to a non-Christian area said, "It is difficult to win these people to faith in Jesus, because most preachers and teachers try to argue with them. This never works. Only those believers who accept them, respect them, and make them feel loved manage to exert any influence at all." Criticisms and prohibitions threaten people and cause them to hold on to their positions more firmly than ever. Acceptance and affirmation will relieve the pressure and allow them to change their beliefs and behavior voluntarily.

By analyzing Jesus's gospel we've learned that his teachings dealt with affirming the positive rather than condemning the negative. He was able to emphasize this important characteristic by separating truth from tradition.

Chapter 3

It's Personalized, Not Standardized

"The Sabbath was made for humankind and not humankind for the Sabbath." (Mark 2:27)

Jesus assures us that the rules and commandments of religion were given to benefit ordinary men and women. They were not arbitrary requirements instigated by an authoritarian god.

Jeremiah understood this: "Surely I know the plans I have for you, says the LORD, plans for your welfare and not for harm, to give you a future with hope. Then when you call upon me and come and pray to me, I will hear you. When you search for me, you will find me; if you seek me with all your heart" (Jer 29:11–13).

This promise is important because all of us need a benevolent creator and a loving father. All of us are seeking contentment and fulfillment. All of us are looking for an instant happiness kit. All of us are hoping for a quick fix. All of us want to discover and follow three simple steps for a peace insurance plan. All of us desire a procedure guaranteed to solve our problems. All of us are waiting for some divine instructor to say, "Complete this simple form and you'll possess life abundant!" Unfortunately, there are no universal panaceas. There are no one-size-fits-all solutions.

When we examine Jesus's style and ministry, the third characteristic we notice is that he avoided prescribed formulas. Instead, he offered a personalized approach to salvation and abundant life.

In witnessing situations, Jesus did not do what many traditional Christians feel obligated to do. He didn't give a list of requirements. He didn't describe a definite set of beliefs. He didn't follow a predetermined plan. In fact, he almost never initiated an evangelistic encounter. When asked, his explanations often seem incomplete and at times contradictory. A few of his statements do indicate that to believe is enough. Once, when some people asked him, "'What must we do to perform the works of God?' Jesus answered them, 'This is the work of God, that you believe in him whom he has sent'" (John 6:28–29).

Other responses indicate that productive behavior is essential. Jesus said, "The hour is coming when all who are in their graves will hear his voice and will come out: those who have done good to the resurrection of life, and those who have done evil to the resurrection of condemnation" (John 5:28–29).

Quite often Jesus says, "We must believe in his name." In the Bible, the word *name* didn't mean just a title. A person's name was an indication of his character, function, relationship, or destiny. The choice of a name was significant. People were given descriptive designations. Then these descriptions were changed if the individual's basic nature or role changed. That's why Abram became Abraham, Jacob became Israel, Simon became Peter, and Saul became Paul.

This explanation helps us understand the scripture that says, "There is salvation in no one else, for there is no other name under heaven given among mortals by which we must be saved" (Acts 4:12). This verse is based on the firm conviction that Jesus exemplified the essence of truth. He said, "I am the way the truth and the life." If so, then of course there is no other or different or contradictory name that will ensure us of having an abundant, eternal life. It's also obvious that anyone who exemplifies Jesus's character and follows his principles is "of Christ" whether he wears the label or not (see Matt 25:31–40).

This definition of the term *name* also clarifies the scripture that says, "Go therefore and make disciples of all nations, baptizing them in the name of the Father and of the Son and of the Holy Spirit" (Matt 28:19).

For converts to submerge themselves in their new spiritual lives, they must emulate the nature of God, obey the teachings of Jesus, and follow the guidance of the Holy Spirit.

These antithetical admonitions can cause considerable confusion unless we realize that Jesus's interviews were individualized. He made no blanket pronouncements. He offered no universal solutions. Instead, he counseled each person differently.

Nicodemus was confused about physical and spiritual existence. So he received enlightenment concerning new beginnings for Jews as well as for gentiles. Jesus said, "I tell you, no one can see the kingdom of God without being born from above" (John 3:3).

The thief on the cross simply needed reassurance. So Jesus said, "Truly I tell you, today you will be with me in paradise" (Luke 23:43).

Now, if conversions are matters of life or death, and especially if they are matters of heaven or hell, why didn't Jesus go through all the same proper steps on each occasion? Orthodox witnessers would feel that a person was derelict in his duty if he failed to give complete instructions to each inquirer. Some moralists would accuse a person of being negligent if he didn't press for a decision at every opportunity.

It's significant that even though Jesus spent his entire ministry with people, you can never find him advocating one exact process by which you can "put in a token of faith and get out a ticket to heaven." He loved people! He served people! He yearned for people! Yet he never gave anyone a brief formula that would automatically bestow everlasting life.

If a person only needs to acknowledge and accept a vicarious atonement theory, then it seems strange that Jesus failed to mention it. Yet he didn't really discuss that subject with anybody. For instance, when Jesus met the Syrophoenician woman, she was concerned about her child's health. He explored her attitude on racial matters and respected her quick wit. Then he compassionately responded to her need (see Mark 7:25–30). But why didn't he pursue the matter of her eternal salvation? She seemed to be receptive. The time was surely right. Yet there is no evidence that he explained the doctrine of redemption or invited her to embrace a Messianic-oriented ideology.

When the Roman centurion requested help for his servant, Jesus was gracious. He extended mercy and even expressed surprise and admiration at the Roman's great faith (see Luke 7:2–9). But faith in what? Did this foreigner understand the Jewish expectation of a spiritual deliverer? Did he know the prophecies about the sacrificial atonement? Did he trust Jesus's future propitiation for the forgiveness of his sins? There is no evidence that he did. This was surely a golden opportunity for witnessing. Why didn't Jesus take advantage of it?

In telling the story of the good Samaritan, Jesus did not evaluate the orthodoxy of the man's beliefs. He only commended the righteousness of his actions (see Luke 10:30–37). Now, according to Jewish theology, Samaritans were practically heretics. They held many paganistic notions. In no way could they be considered true believers.

If contending for the faith and maintaining pure doctrine is so important, why didn't Jesus add a few lines to his account, making it perfectly clear that this particular Samaritan he had praised was a converted disciple with full knowledge of saving grace? Instead, Jesus honored his concern for others and complimented his practical deeds of service. He presented him as a hero but utterly ignored the vital area of his salvation. No mention is made of his relationship with the Lord. As far as we know, there was no death, burial, or resurrection teachings in his faith system. Why did Jesus leave the impression that having a good neighbor policy is more important than having your soul right with God?

In encounter after encounter, we see Jesus either neglecting the subject of salvation altogether or giving incomplete and conflicting information on how it is to be attained.

If Jesus knew what was best and used the most effective approach, we must assume that salvation is much more complex than we have realized. A salvation experience must include a sense of personal value and a belief in God's grace. No single canned procedure will produce such an awareness in every person. With more than seven thousand languages in the world today, no single expression can speak to everybody. With more than sixteen thousand distinct cultural groups in the world today, no brief explanation can effect change in all of them.

It's interesting that the rich young ruler and the Philippian jailer each asked essentially the same question. One said, "What must I do to inherit eternal life?" (Mark 10:17). The other said, "What must I do to be saved?" (Acts 16:30). The responses given to these questions, however, were radically different. The rich young ruler's problem seemed to lie in the areas of priorities and stewardship. The scriptures say, "A man ran up and knelt before [Jesus] and asked him, 'Good Teacher, what must I do to inherit eternal life?'" After discussing the Ten Commandments, Jesus looked at him, loved him, and said, "You lack one thing; go, sell what you own, and give the money to the poor, and you will have treasure in heaven; then come, follow me" (see Mark 10:17–22).

Paul, on the other hand, quickly answered the jailer with a brief formula: "Believe in the Lord Jesus, and you will be saved" (Acts 16:31). Now, if there is really one correct procedure that everyone must follow, then why are these replies so different? Perhaps by the time the subject of salvation had filtered down to Paul, the description of the process had been reduced to a simple formula.

The approach Jesus used, however, was much more flexible. Many of the people he met were from diverse cultural backgrounds, and some of them had not been instructed in Hebrew theology. Therefore, leading all of them through the carefully prescribed steps of realizing their sin, repenting, accepting Jesus as their savior, and making a public confession of faith would have been inappropriate and confusing.

Of course, the Jews of that time and place had been especially steeped in the sacrificial atonement tradition. For centuries their spiritual condition had depended upon altars, burnt offerings, and blood sacrifices. They were superstitious and fearful. Guilt was a heavy burden. They had been conditioned to believe that expiation or propitiation was imperative for forgiveness. They were slaves to ceremonies and laws. They desperately needed feelings of forgiveness and assurances of personal worth.

We need to realize, however, that the phrases and explanations that were meaningful and perhaps even necessary for people at that time and place can become stilted, empty, and confusing when forced upon twenty-first-century Americans. Witnesses today must give a more meaningful and relevant explanation. We should never leave the impression that you can get into heaven by knowing the right combination to the pearly gates or that salvation can be received by using the proper password.

The gospel must be understood. The gospel must be internalized. The gospel must be personalized. There is no universal formula that will be successful with every person. Whatever it takes to make you realize that God accepts and loves you is what's necessary for your salvation. Whatever it takes to make you believe in your own personal worth is what's necessary for your salvation. Whatever it takes to help you develop your own potential to the fullest is what's necessary for your salvation.

It's obvious that no single set of abstract requirements will accomplish this profound psychological transformation for everybody. Thus, an effective plan of salvation will of necessity vary from one person to another. Each of us has a different background. Each of us has developed different hangups. Each of us has different internal conflicts. That's why salvation experiences are so different. When they are converted, some people have dramatic emotional catharses; others only have a quiet sense of commitment. But both can be totally valid.

There was a striking absence of dogmatic pontification in Jesus's ministry. He was primarily concerned with individuals, not with groups. More of his time was spent in personal conversation than in public oration. He knew that very little of spiritual import is accomplished by mass communication and wholesale admonitions.

Each person has his own weak areas. Each person has his own ego injuries. Each person has his own blind spots. These problems require counseling on a one-to-one basis. Salvation can't be acquired "off the rack," so to speak. It must be "tailor made"!

Jesus knew the power of belief is tremendous. He knew it can achieve great benefits or be a great hindrance. If you believe in ghosts, then a white sheet on a dark night can cause drastic changes in your mind and body! It can even increase your heart rate and blood pressure. But if you don't believe in ghosts, then that white sheet will have no effect on you at all. That's the power of belief!

If you glimpse a garden hose and believe it's a snake, then you may have a panic attack or even a heart attack! That's the power of belief!

If a telemarketer claims you have just won the lottery, you'll probably have no reaction. But if someone you trust tells you, you'll have a positive reaction. That's the power of belief!

You can legally own a large inheritance for many years, but you'll never use it or enjoy it unless you know about it and believe you own it. This same thing is true of salvation.

Primitive people thought gods were wrathful and eager to punish them if they broke a rule. Therefore, they tried to please God with sacrifices and worship. They were wrong! Instead, our God made us in his image and blessed us (see Gen 1:27–28). He loves us and wants to know us.

Salvation is a given. We don't have to fulfill any requirements to obtain it. It's already ours. The scripture says, "Just as one man's trespass led to condemnation for all, so one man's act of righteousness leads to justification and life for all" (Rom 5:18). Another scripture says, "We have our hope set on the living God, who is the Savior of all people, especially of those who believe" (1 Tim 4:10).

Belief is an activating word. That's why, in the scriptures, the word *believe* is used repeatedly. Jesus urged people to "believe in the good news" (Mark 1:15).

Once, when two blind men asked him for help, Jesus said, "Do you have faith that I can do this?" When they said, "Yes, Lord," Jesus touched them and said, "According to your faith let it be done to you" (Matt 9:28–29). And it was. He also said, "All things can be done for the one who believes" (Mark 9:23).

When Jesus healed someone, he never said, "God has performed this miracle" or "My special ability has cured your disease." Instead, he said, "Your faith has made you whole." In short, he was saying, "You are the only one who can solve this problem." If you believe you're worthless, you'll become worthless. If you believe you're unproductive, you'll become unproductive. If you believe you're evil, you'll become evil. On the other hand, if you believe you're worthy, you'll become worthy. If you believe you're productive, you'll become productive. If you believe you're good, you'll become good. That's the power of belief!

Jesus always let people voice their own needs and express their own concerns. He listened and affirmed their worth. It's also surprising that he often had only one encounter with people seeking help. Were these brief conversations enough to effect a lasting transformation? It would be interesting to do a follow-up study to determine what they were doing a month, a year, or a decade later. It seems his method was to plant seeds of truth and then trust that growth would continue. He was committed to the idea that grace and love can work miracles in human lives.

Salvation means becoming whole. It means being restored to a state of health. It motivates us to make necessary changes in our behavior. It enables us to reach our optimum potential. Salvation describes a quality of life. It's infinitely more complex than the traditional view suggests. A Bible scholar reported, "As I studied the scriptures, I was surprised to find that in Jesus's teachings he had a lot more to say about 'living it' than he did about 'getting it'!"

Most people want an instant transformation without having to face any difficulties or endure any hardships. They're like the old deacon whose standard prayer was, "Oh, Lord, deliver us from the trials of life and get us into heaven at last." That's not salvation. The trials are part of the process. They provide the shaping, the learning, and the growing that stimulate and support the spiritual transformation! The scripture tells us that even Jesus was made perfect by his sufferings (see Heb 2:10).

Each of us must develop our own unique Christlikeness. As individuals, each of us must discover and express our own ideology and complete our own life puzzle. Others can help us find the pieces, but we must put them together for ourselves!

By analyzing Jesus's gospel, we've learned that his teachings dealt with a personalized approach to religion and salvation, rather than relying on a standardized system. He was able to emphasize this important characteristic by separating truth from tradition.

Section 2

Principles of the Gospel

Chapter 4

God Is in Believers

"You are God's temple...God's Spirit dwells in you." (1 Cor 3:16)

Our analysis has shown that the gospel does not give specific answers to trivial questions. It does not list absolute prohibitions or set forth rigid rules. It does not present one concise universal formula for salvation. What, then, is the good news? What is the gospel?

When asked this question, many people immediately reply, "The gospel is the death, burial, and resurrection of Jesus!" If that's true, then Jesus didn't preach the gospel! His allusions to these coming events were veiled at best. He didn't present them forcefully enough to even convince his own followers. Peter, one of the inner circle, protested vehemently when Jesus mentioned such a possibility: "Jesus began to show his disciples that he must go to Jerusalem and undergo great suffering at the hands of the elders and chief priests and scribes and be killed and on the third day be raised. And Peter took him aside and began to rebuke him, saying, 'God forbid it, Lord! This must never happen to you'" (Matt 16:21–22).

If the gospel is the death, burial, and resurrection, then the disciples certainly didn't preach the gospel when they were sent out on their first mission. Instead, they spoke about the kingdom and healed people. The scriptures say, "[Jesus] sent them out to proclaim the kingdom of God and to heal the sick.... They departed and went through the villages, bringing the good news and curing diseases everywhere" (Luke 9:2, 6).

In fact, they were totally unaware of his impending death, and we know they never expected a resurrection because none of them waited at the tomb for three days.

The preaching of the gospel during Jesus's own ministry included very little information about deaths and resurrections. This theme developed later from Peter's sermon on the day of Pentecost and Paul's letters. The doctrine of a vicarious atonement was emphasized after the fact to give meaning to Jesus's crucifixion.

The gospel, as proclaimed by Jesus himself, was not theoretical or doctrinal. Rather, it had an immediate and practical relevance. A careful study reveals that he presented three dynamic, life-changing principles.

The first and most important principle is that God lives in the hearts of believers! Jesus revolutionized the concept of God, changing him from a ruler into a Father. A tyrannical deity out there became a loving Spirit in here. That's what incarnation means—God in the flesh, God in human beings, God in us! Even the people in the first century realized the wonderful possibilities inherent in this claim. Once, when a paralytic was healed, "[The crowd] was filled with awe, and they glorified God, who had given such authority to human beings" (Matt 9:8).

Jesus said, "The Father is in me and I am in the Father" (John 10:38), but that by itself is not particularly good news. The good news part is that God is in all believers, not just in Jesus. Later, it's surprising that John's acid test for Christianity did not lie in a belief about Jesus's divinity, but rather in a belief about Jesus's humanity! That's what was being denied by the Gnostic heretics. It was hard for them to believe that the supreme deity of the universe could live in a lowly earthly species. Therefore, the crucial question was not "Is Jesus really God?" but rather "Is Jesus really a man?" John said, "Beloved, do not believe every spirit, but test the spirits to see whether they are from God, for many false prophets have gone out into the world. By this you know the Spirit of God: every spirit that confesses that Jesus Christ has come in the flesh is from God" (1 John 4:1–2).

The reason this issue is so relevant is that if God can reside in the flesh of one human being, then he can reside in the flesh of all human beings. The gospel stands or falls on this point!

To clarify his message, Jesus presented the spiritual aspects of the gospel, saying, "God is spirit" (John 4:24). If this is true, then divine beings don't reside on mountains or in temples, but rather in the hearts and lives of men and women. If God is Spirit, then worship isn't something that takes place on mountains or in temples, but rather in the hearts and lives of men and women.

This idea has many pertinent implications for us: If we are in Christ and Christ is in God, then we are in God! That's a logical syllogism. If God is in Christ and Christ is in us, then God is in us! That's a logical syllogism. If we and Christ are one and Christ and God are one, then we and God are one! That's another logical syllogism.

Jesus said, "On that day you will know that I am in my Father, and you in me, and I in you" (John 14:20).

If these statements are valid, then what God can do, Jesus can do; what Jesus can do, we can do! The transfer process follows this sequence: God's power, authority, and privileges became Jesus's power, authority, and privileges. Then Jesus's power, authority, and privileges became our power, authority, and privileges. Jesus said, "All things have been handed over to me by my Father, and no one knows the Son except the Father, and no one knows the Father except the Son and anyone to whom the Son chooses to reveal him" (Matt 11:27). Of course, Jesus chose to reveal him to every person who would respond.

Later, he made the chain of command perfectly clear when he said, "As the Father has sent me, so I send you" (John 20:21).

If we are truly one with Jesus, then the terms *Son of Man* and *mankind* are interchangeable. Jesus prayed, "I am no longer in the world, but they are in the world, and I am coming to you. Holy Father, protect them in your name that you have given me, so that they may be one, as we are one" (John 17:11).

When we accept this idea, many scriptures take on a new significance. Jesus's explanation concerning a believer's status and position, as to rights and responsibilities, even include the matter of forgiveness: "The Son of Man has authority on earth to forgive sins" (Matt 9:6).

Jesus claimed this authority for himself, but then he specifically gave this authority to his disciples: "If you forgive the sins of any, they are forgiven them; if you retain the sins of any, they are retained" (John 20:23).

This strange statement doesn't mean all of us have been given God's role of absolution. Instead, it validates the modern psychological principle that people "become as they are treated." As human beings, if we reject and condemn a person as a worthless individual, he often becomes one. If, on the other hand, we accept and affirm a person as a worthwhile individual, he often becomes one!

What we bind is bound, and what we loose is loosed! Jesus said, "I will give you the keys of the kingdom of heaven, and whatever you bind on earth will be bound in heaven, and whatever you loose on earth will be loosed in heaven" (Matt 16:19).

These keys of the kingdom represent a Christian's remarkable ability to effect change and transform people. We can bring out the worst or the best in others. We can literally act for God here on this earth!

The Son of Man or mankind also has authority over rituals, tradition, and worship practices: "The Sabbath was made for humankind and not humankind for the Sabbath, so the Son of Man is lord even of the Sabbath" (Mark 2:27–28).

Again, this means that human beings take precedence over ceremonies. If the Sabbath is for us, then we are justified in concluding that all ceremonies and practices, including religious ones, are established for the welfare of people, not to satisfy God.

As to matters of learning, Jesus said, "It is enough for the disciple to be like the teacher (Matt 10:25). This indicates that in acquiring knowledge, we're free to approach the level of Jesus himself without apology. Anti-intellectualism has been dealt a death blow. It's not sinful to want to know! The old tower of Babel curse is destroyed forever (see Gen 11:4–9). God certainly isn't jealous or threatened by our growth or attainment of wisdom.

To further cinch the matter, John emphasized this theme in his letter, saying, "As he is, so are we in this world" (1 John 4:17).

Sometimes it's hard for people to understand that God is with us. Those who are shallow-thinking and short-sighted often complain about things such as the separation of church and state. They say, "If you can't read the Bible to your students in the public schools, you're taking God out of the classroom. If you can't repeat the Lord's Prayer or include prayers at sports events, you're taking God out of the schools." But that's not true!

God is love. The scripture says, "God is love, and those who abide in love abide in God, and God abides in them" (1 John 4:16). So if you take love into the classroom, then God is there.

God is truth. The scripture says, "The LORD is good…his truth endureth to all generations" (Ps 100:5 KJV). So if you take truth into the classroom, then God is there.

God is righteous. The scripture says, "O LORD God of Israel, thou art righteous" (Ezra 9:15 KJV). So if you take righteousness into the classroom, then God is there.

In fact, as Christians we are God's temples, and God lives in us. The scripture says, "Do you not know that you are God's temple and that God's Spirit dwells in you?" (1 Cor 3:16). Therefore, if a believer goes into a classroom, then God is there!

This is true of all interactions. In social relationships we are stand-ins for Jesus and therefore for God. Jesus said, "Whoever welcomes you welcomes me, and whoever welcomes me welcomes the one who sent me" (Matt 10:40). This is an underrated statement! To paraphrase, Jesus is saying, "He who accepts and honors people accepts and honors me, and thereby they are accepting and honoring God." This clarifies and supports Jesus's remark in the parable of the sheep and goats, when he said, "Just as you did it to one of the least of these…you did it for me" (Matt 25:40).

When we elevate humanity, some people protest that this shows a lack of reverence for God. Jesus, however, defended this evaluation of humanity. Once, when Jesus said, "The Father and I are one," the Jews wanted to stone him. Jesus replied,

> "I have shown you many good works from the Father. For which of these are you going to stone me?" The Jews answered, "It is not for a good work that we are going to stone you but for blasphemy, because you, though only a human being, are making yourself God." Jesus answered, "Is it not written in your law, 'I said, you are

> gods'? If those to whom the word of God came were called 'gods'—and the scripture cannot be annulled—can you say that the one whom the Father has sanctified and sent into the world is blaspheming because I said, 'I am God's Son'?" (John 10:33–36)

Some people say, "Oh, but the only one who can claim such divine sanctification is Jesus." He's the one "whom the Father sanctified and sent into the world." But that quotation in the book of Psalms certainly didn't mean Jesus. It was plural and adds the phrase "You are gods, children of the Most High, all of you" (Ps 82:6).

Jesus specifically claimed this role for his followers in a prayer, saying, "Sanctify them in the truth; your word is truth. As you have sent me into the world, so I have sent them into the world. And for their sakes I sanctify myself, so that they also may be sanctified in truth" (John 17:17–19).

This is the heart of the gospel! Individual men and women are of supreme worth! They have inalienable rights and unlimited possibilities.

To twenty-first-century Americans this may not sound revolutionary since our democracy is based upon these very principles, but to first-century Palestinians it was a bombshell. Historically, life was cheap. Human beings were considered expendable in tribal endeavors such as war. Even human sacrifice had once been acceptable. Human slavery was still acceptable. All people except kings, priests, and very wealthy individuals were assigned an inferior status, and certain groups were assigned an even lower status. Women had less worth. The children, the poor, the handicapped, and foreigners had less worth. At best, only rich, healthy, male Jews could really be considered first-class citizens of the kingdom of God.

The gospel changed that. If each unique soul has a divine spark, then each has an eternal significance. The gospel emphasizes value. It says we are of more value than birds: "Are not five sparrows sold for two pennies? Yet not one of them is forgotten in God's sight.... Do not be afraid; you are of more value than many sparrows" (Luke 12:6–7).

We are of more value than animals: "Suppose one of you has only one sheep and it falls into a pit on the Sabbath; will you not lay hold of it and lift it out? How much more valuable is a human being than a sheep!" (Matt 12:11–12).

We are of more value than a world full of things: "What will it profit them if they gain the whole world but forfeit their life? Or what will they give in return for their life?" (Matt 16:26).

We are valuable because God is in us! In primitive times traits such as authority, knowledge, and strength were considered "of the gods." Jesus's gospel assures us that ordinary people also have a right to these traits.

The role and mission of Christians are some of the most misunderstood concepts of religion. We are not slaves. Instead, we are totally autonomous. We are in control. The scripture says God blessed men and women and said, "Have dominion over the fish of the sea and over the birds of the air and over every living thing that moves upon the earth" (Gen 1:28).

The psalmist said, "The heavens are the LORD's heavens, but the earth he has given to human beings" (Ps 115:16).

We are not immature children. Instead, we are mature sons and daughters of God. We're equal to Jesus in every respect. He said, "Whoever does the will of God is my brother and sister and mother" (Mark 3:35).

Jesus said we have his ability: "The one who believes in me will also do the works that I do and, in fact, will do greater works than these" (John 14:12). We even have the same access and relationship to God that Jesus has. He said, "I do not say to you that I will ask the Father on your behalf, for the Father himself loves you" (John 16:26–27).

We are more than servants; we are friends, agents, and ambassadors for God. We are authorized to represent and speak for him. Jesus said, "I do not call you servants any longer, because the servant does not know what the master is doing, but I have called you friends, because I have made known to you everything that I have heard from my Father" (John 15:14–15).

In fact, we are living images of God. He specifically said, "Let us make humans in our image, according to our likeness.... God created humans in his image, in the image of God he created them; male and female he created them" (Gen 1:26–27). Few people realize this important principle because too many churches teach that we are depraved, worthless sinners.

Most religions believe Christians fill roles and have responsibilities exactly opposite to biblical views. We can't fulfill our purpose if we think we are sinful creatures put here on earth to obey and worship a spiritual monarch. Jesus taught that we are his valuable, responsible, productive coworkers. This belief does great things for people's self-esteem. It increases their confidence and improves their attitudes.

Once, a naughty little boy was constantly in trouble. He always lost his homework and failed his academic tests. He was intelligent but extremely careless and negligent. One day, his teacher scolded him severely. She said, "Johnny, you are very smart! You could be the best student in this class if you would just listen and do your best!" His eyes were big and serious when he looked at her and said, "Teacher, I didn't know that!" Afterward, this child made remarkable progress and eventually became a successful businessman. A tremendous change begins to come over any individual when they understand for the first time that they have real worth and are in a legitimate position of power.

In mythology, there is the recurring theme of mortals who are given special status from the gods. If these individuals can become convinced that they have the ability to do heroic feats, then they can do them! It all depends upon their state of mind and their belief in themselves. Sometimes a talisman or invisible armor was bestowed to increase confidence. As long as the individuals had these aids, or thought they had them, they were invincible! Of course, that's the crux of the matter. The object itself doesn't make them strong. Instead, it's their belief in the object that makes them strong! Ability depends on confidence.

In fairy tales, there is also the recurring theme of captive members of royalty who don't know their true identity. If these individuals can become convinced of their status as true princes and princesses, then they can exert the necessary authority to overcome their bonds and take their rightful position. It all depends on their state of mind and their belief in themselves. Again, ability depends on confidence.

The gospel also has a recurring theme. It says all believers are given special power from God. All men and women can have the status of princes and princesses, and if they just believe this, success is theirs. Ability comes with confidence, and confidence means "with faith."

By analyzing Jesus's gospel, we've learned that his teachings dealt with the idea that God is a loving spirit in believers, rather than a vengeful deity sitting on a throne somewhere. He was able to emphasize this revolutionary principle by separating truth from tradition.

Chapter 5

Power Is in Truth

"The truth will make you free." (John 8:32)

Jesus didn't promote his message by means of superstition. He didn't appeal to fears. He didn't use threats. He didn't quote authorities. He didn't depend on tradition. He dared to declare that something isn't right just because men of old said so. Something isn't right just because a majority of the people think so. Instead, something is right because it's right! Isn't that amazing?

Therefore, the second principle delineated in Jesus's gospel is that power is in truth.

Jesus transferred the concept of authority from heaven to earth. He changed its base from monarchs and armies to integrity and reality. He said, "Truth, not armor, makes us invincible!" This idea has many pertinent implications for us. It's significant that *truth* and *Christ* are synonymous. He said, "I am the way and the truth and the life" (John 14:6).

Truth was Jesus's watch word. Propagating truth was Jesus's purpose. He said, "'For this I was born, and for this I came into the world, to testify to the truth. Everyone who belongs to the truth listens to my voice.' Pilate asked him, 'What is truth?'" (John 18:37–38).

Many of us can identify with Pilate's question. It's one of the most important questions we'll ever confront. *Truth* is an abstract term that's often used carelessly and imprecisely, but it represents a vital principle.

Truth in the biblical context meant open and candid, not false. Truth, by Webster's definition, means the established facts that are real and actual. Truth is what is! Jehovah identified himself to Moses with the immortal words, "I AM WHO I AM" (Exod 3:14). When he said this, he was equating himself with the reality of the universe. He was claiming the name of truth!

Jesus exemplified, taught, and practiced truth. Furthermore, he emphasized the scientific method of ascertaining truth. In his teachings he urged the use of reason and analogy. His criteria was not, "You will know them by their reputation" or "You will know them by their sincerity," or "You will know them by their orthodoxy," but rather, "You will know them by their fruits" (Matt 7:20). Now, fruits are visible, tangible, and concrete. For Jesus, the proof of the pudding was in the eating!

Jesus never asked people to observe a tradition or accept a belief on the basis of some ethereal revelation. He never once said, "Brethren, I've had a vision! So you'd better follow me" or "Brethren, the Lord has laid this on my heart! So you'd better listen to me!" Instead, he said, "Observe my works. Look at the evidence. Analyze the results." The scriptures say, "When John heard in prison what the Messiah was doing, he sent word by his disciples and said to him, 'Are you one who is to come, or are we to wait for another?'" (Matt 11:2–3).

Now, if ever anyone deserved a straightforward, absolute answer, it was John. He had been imprisoned and was awaiting death. From the depth of depression and doubt he pleaded for assurance. Yet, even under these circumstances Jesus maintained his emphasis on inductive reasoning. The scriptures say, "Jesus answered them, 'Go and tell John what you hear and see: the blind receive their sight, the lame walk, those with a skin disease are cleansed, the deaf hear, the dead are raised, and the poor have good news brought to them'" (Matt 11:4–5).

Over and over, Jesus urged us to believe on the basis of what we see and hear. He said, "If I am not doing the works of my Father, then do not believe me. But if I do them, even though you do not believe me, believe the works, so that you may know and understand that the Father is in me and I am in the Father" (John 10:37–38).

This was an unusual and challenging statement. Most religious spokesmen try to prove their authority by describing how God has spoken to them in dreams or appeared to them in miraculous visions, but Jesus simply said, "If I'm expressing God's love through my actions, that's enough credentials for anyone! If you can't see divine purposes in my words and deeds, then it would be impossible for you to recognize them anywhere!" Some circumstances are so strong they need no support. Some things are self-evident! Jesus was saying, "Truth speaks for itself!"

Truth enables, disciplines. and evaluates. In the overall sense, God doesn't judge us; Satan doesn't judge us; people don't judge us. It's truth that judges us! Jesus said, "The one who rejects me and does not receive my words has a judge; on the last day the word that I have spoken will serve as judge" (John 12:48).

This "word" is *logos* or embodied wisdom. It is reason or reality! It is truth! Our deeds are ultimately judged by their consequences. Our actions are judged by their results. In short, we are ultimately judged by life itself, and you can't fool Mother Nature!

Paul said, "Do not be deceived; God is not mocked, for you reap whatever you sow" (Gal 6:7). That's the power of truth! Shakespeare said, "To thine own self be true; then it follow as the night the day; thou canst not be false to any man!" That is such an important admonition. Above all, we must be true to ourselves.

Jesus repeatedly warned people to be genuine and authentic. He condemned hypocrites, saying, "Beware of false prophets, who come to you in sheep's clothing but inwardly are ravenous wolves" (Matt 7:15). He also said, "Woe to you, scribes and Pharisees, hypocrites! For you are like whitewashed tombs, which on the outside look beautiful but inside are full of the bones of the dead and of all kinds of uncleanness" (Matt 23:27).

Evaluating ourselves is a vital matter. We must be honest as we develop our self-image and estimate our self-esteem. This includes analyzing our strengths and weaknesses, our abilities and disabilities, our beliefs and opinions and our purposes. These things determine our moral character and our productivity. For instance, if we believe we're bad, then doing a bad deed seems reasonable and causes no dissonance. But if we believe we're valuable children of God, doing a bad deed feels wrong, and our conscience will urge us to change our actions and repent.

Traditionally, superstition often takes precedence over reality. Illogical, unrelated incidents were often linked to establish fantastic theories of cause and effect. For example, primitive people concluded that taking a census caused a plague. The scriptures say, "David was stricken to the heart because he had numbered the people. David said to the LORD, 'I have sinned greatly in what I have done.'... So the LORD sent a pestilence on Israel...and seventy thousand of the people died" (2 Sam 24:10, 15).

Primitive people concluded that immorality caused volcanos. The scriptures say, "Then the men said to Lot...'We are about to destroy this place, because the outcry against its people has become great before the LORD, and the LORD has sent us to destroy it.' Then the LORD rained on Sodom and Gomorrah sulfur and fire from the LORD out of heaven" (Gen 19:12–13, 24).

Primitive people concluded that adultery caused infant mortality. After David sinned with Bathsheba, the scripture says, "Because by this deed you have utterly scorned the LORD, the child born to you shall die" (2 Sam 12:14).

Primitive people concluded that idolatry and disobedience caused military defeats. The scriptures say,

> They abandoned the house of the LORD, the God of their ancestors, and served the sacred poles and the idols. And wrath came upon Judah and Jerusalem for this guilt of theirs. Then the spirit of God took possession of Zechariah...he stood above the people and said to them, "Because you have forsaken the LORD, he has also forsaken you."... At the end of the year, the army of Aram came...to Judah and Jerusalem and destroyed all the officials of the people.... Although the army of Aram had come with few men, the LORD delivered into their hand a very great army because they had abandoned the LORD. (2 Chron 24:18, 20, 23–24)

Primitive people concluded that sinful behavior caused droughts. The scripture says, "Heavens is shut up and there is no rain because they have sinned against you" (1 Kgs 8:35).

Primitive people concluded that divine anger caused storms. The scriptures say, "His adversaries will be shattered; the Most High will thunder in heaven.... I will call upon the LORD, that he may send thunder and rain, and you shall know and see that the wickedness that you have done in the sight of the LORD is great" (1 Sam 2:10; 12:17).

Primitive people concluded that burning an animal carcass caused God to change his mind and improve his mood. The scriptures say, "Then Noah built an altar to the LORD and took of every clean animal and of every clean bird and offered burnt offerings on the altar. And when the LORD smelled the pleasing odor, the LORD said in his heart, 'I will never again curse the ground because of humans...nor will I ever again destroy every living creature as I have done'" (Gen 8:20–21).

All in all, superstition reigned supreme. Truth was an unknown quantity. Jesus moved religion an enormous step forward by linking consequences to their actual causes. Jesus taught that people should judge things by visual fruits or practical results instead of by irrational fears, ancient taboos, rituals, and ceremonies. He said, "You will know them by their fruits. Are grapes gathered from thorns or figs from thistles? In the same way, every good tree bears good fruit, but the bad tree bears bad fruit" (Matt 7:16–17). He advised us to adapt our lifestyle to what works, not to what authoritative decrees or traditional habits demand.

If you read between the lines, you'll find that Jesus ridiculed many well-known and revered beliefs and practices, such as that of making long prayers and fasting. He said, "When you are praying, do not heap up empty phrases as the gentiles do, for they think that they will be heard because of their many words.... And whenever you fast, do not look somber, like the hypocrites, for they mark their faces to show others that they are fasting. Truly I tell you, they have received their reward" (Matt 6:7, 16).

He even scorned those who made "their phylacteries broad and their fringes long" to impress people with their pious behavior (see Matt 23:5). Phylacteries were little boxes of scripture that they wore on their foreheads, and the fringes were on their prayer shawls.

Jesus was constantly challenging the status quo. He often replaced old commandments with his own advice. One of his most controversial statements was, "You have heard that it was said…but I say to you…" (see Matt 5:38–44).

Several of these quotes from ancient times that he repudiated were from Old Testament passages, supposedly dictated by God. Such a contradiction of scripture was unheard of! Such a rejection of tradition was unheard of! Such a display of courage was unheard of! Yet Jesus took the risk because he felt truth must be proclaimed at any cost! The cost to him was death! When we try to speak truth to unwilling people, we must always be open and honest about our own beliefs. We can't hide our natural temperaments, and we can't wear a mask. We must accept responsibility and never play the blame game. When the prodigal son got home, the first thing he said was, "I have sinned. No one is to blame but me."

Now he could have said, "My father was too indulgent. He shouldn't have given me all my inheritance. He knew I would waste it." He could have said, "It was my brother's fault. He's so jealous. He made me miserable."

Instead, he said, "No, it's not my father. It's not my brother. It's not my home situation. I'm to blame for this predicament."

The scripture says, "Each of us will be accountable to God" (see Rom 14:12).

It's easy to avoid accountability by denying, distorting, or distracting. When we're dealing with people who have ulterior motives, we must be vigilant. Opponents may want to win. Salesmen may want our money. Politicians may want our votes. Jesus said, "Don't be gullible": "Be wise as serpents and innocent as doves" (Matt 10:16).

It's important for our communication to be clear and personal. We should use "I" language to describe how we really feel and to explain what we really want. We should say things like, "I really care about you" or "I feel hurt when you ignore me." Communication is more about feelings than facts. Our speech must reveal both.

Unfortunately, many people prefer pleasant delusions to unpleasant truth. They literally refuse to hear things that contradict their belief systems. They will even destroy the messenger if they don't like the message. This happens whenever honest thinkers dare to speak out. It happened to the prophets before Jesus came. He said, "You testify against yourselves that you are descendants of those who murdered the prophets" (Matt 23:31).

It happened to Stephen after Jesus came. The scriptures say, "They covered their ears, and with a loud shout all rushed together against him. Then they dragged him out of the city and began to stone him" (Acts 7:57–58).

Jesus himself was the target of violence on many occasions. The first recorded incident was in his hometown of Nazareth when he reminded them that non-Jews were accepted and especially blessed by God while many orthodox Jews were overlooked. The scriptures say, "There were many widows in Israel in the time of Elijah, when…there was a severe famine over all the land, yet Elijah was sent to none of them except to a widow at Zarephath in Sidon. There were also many with a skin disease in Israel in the time of the prophet Elisha, and none of them was cleansed except Naaman the Syrian" (Luke 4:25–27).

The people became critical again when Jesus claimed personal autonomy and refused to submit to their rule-oriented belief system. The scriptures say,

> At that time Jesus went through the grain fields on the Sabbath; his disciples were hungry, and they began to pluck heads of grain and to eat. When the Pharisees saw it, they said to him, "Look, your disciples are doing what is not lawful to do on the Sabbath." He said to them, "Have you not read what David did when he and his companions were hungry? How he entered the house of God, and they ate the bread of the Presence, which it was not lawful for him or his companions to eat, but only for the priests? Or have you not read in the law that on the Sabbath the priests in the temple break the Sabbath and yet are guiltless? I tell you, something greater than the temple is here. But if you had known what this means, 'I desire mercy and not sacrifice,' you would not have condemned the guiltless. For the Son of Man is lord of the Sabbath." (Matt 12:1–8)

The people began to plot Jesus's death when he elevated the physical needs of hurting people above religious rules and rituals. Once, when he healed a man on the Sabbath day, the scripture says, "The Pharisees went out and conspired against him, how to destroy him" (Matt 12:14).

Believing that God loves everybody and putting people's needs over commandments and traditions were some of the truths that had been missing from the doctrines of the priests, scribes, and Pharisees. These proselytizers had not been reasoning with truth. Rather, they had been indoctrinating with superstition. They had been perpetuating a deadly system of mental slavery. None of their followers would ever become autonomous and self-directed because they had been brainwashed to obey rather than think. They had been conditioned to mindlessly perform ceremonies and follow prescribed regulations. They had turned all their spiritual decisions over to priests and scribes and totally abdicated their rightful positions as sons and daughters of God.

We have to earn the right to independence before we can occupy that role. We have to deserve freedom before we can experience it. We have to be capable of handling a democracy before we can have one.

There are many enemies of truth. Propaganda is dangerous. It can radicalize and condition large groups of people in short periods of time. It deals with simple, concrete issues that everyone can understand. It is repetitious with a few clear points. It is emotional and appeals to feelings. It insists there is only one absolutely right view on every issue. Propaganda doesn't allow any discussions or questions.

An uninformed populace is another enemy of truth. People with a "victim mentality" often have grievances. Sometimes they lack both empathy and common sense. They need approval and often look for a strong hero to revere and follow.

Jesus knew many men and women were vulnerable, so he said, "I am sending you out like lambs into the midst of wolves" (Luke 10:3).

Christians need to realize that God created our brains! Thinking, questioning, and doubting are not sins! Jeremiah, Hosea, and Amos questioned many of the doctrines and belief systems of their time. Jesus was also a constant questioner.

Many people believe false doctrines are those doctrines with which they disagree. But if civilization had listened to correct doctrine advocates, we'd still believe in a flat earth and live in caves.

Some people think if they can just persuade enough people to believe something, that will make it so. But of course it won't! If a million people believe the world is flat, it won't be any flatter than if nobody believed it was flat. Our views about the subject are irrelevant. Facts are stubborn, and they are unconcerned about human beings' opinions. It's easy to stir the public with fear tactics. It's easy to make the masses believe excited crowds and loud voices are synonymous with truth, but they aren't!

Truth also requires more than just correct facts. Once, a teacher asked a little boy, "What does your father do?" He answered, "He shaves every morning." Now, that fact was correct, but it didn't express the truth because it missed the point of the question. The psalmist said, "[God] desire[s] truth in the inward being" (Ps 51:6).

Maturity and responsibility are essential, but only knowledge, understanding, and courage enable men and women to reach that level.

By analyzing Jesus's gospel, we've learned that his teachings dealt with the idea that power is in truth rather than commandments and orthodoxy. He was able to emphasize this revolutionary principle by separating truth from tradition.

Chapter 6

The Kingdom Is Among Us

"The kingdom of God is among you." (Luke 17:21)

Golden slippers on golden streets appeal to a materially deprived society. Safe arms and peaceful rivers appeal to an insecure society. Bountiful harvests and lavish feasts appeal to a starving society. It's evident that both groups and individuals shape their ideas of heaven to fit the gaps in their current earthly existence. We long for a heavenly abode that will give us the things we need in our worldly role. All these models and images of paradise give inadequate and distorted impressions.

Dealing with transcendental and immortal matters requires a high level of spiritual perception. To make things even more complicated, the phrases *eternal life* and *kingdom of God* are sometimes used interchangeably in the Gospels (see Luke 18:29–30). As a result, subjects as diverse as punishments, rewards, and white throne judgments become entangled in our conception of Jesus's idea of the kingdom. Even the prayer "Thy kingdom come on earth as it is in heaven" merges the two realms into a blur.

Jesus revolutionized the concept of the kingdom by moving it from the material future into the spiritual present, but questions remained. He describes it as ethical and internal, not military and external. It seems to have an ideal atmosphere that reveals how life would be if everyone was unselfish and generous. It shows how pleasant life would be if people were concerned for each other. It demonstrates what a productive society we would have if all the inhabitants were knowledgeable and industrious. In fact, this kingdom would really be a foretaste of heaven on earth.

He also eliminated the idea of a physical bailout at some future mystical day of the Lord. His description of the kingdom clearly explains that it doesn't just involve the next world! It also involves this world! It is now, and it is personal!

Therefore, the third principle delineated in Jesus's gospel is that the kingdom is among us. Some translations even say it's within us.

This kingdom that Jesus envisioned had immediate relevance. He said, "As you go, proclaim the good news, 'the kingdom of heaven has come near.'… When they persecute you in this town, flee to the next, for truly I tell you, you will not have finished going through all the towns of Israel before the Son of Man comes" (Matt 10:7, 23).

This statement assures us that he was not referring to some event that was going to be established thousands of years in the future. This kingdom was nearby. Jesus said, "Repent, for the kingdom of heaven has come near" (Matt 4:17). He also said, "Truly I tell you, there are some standing here who will not taste death before they see the kingdom of God" (Luke 9:27). He said, "The kingdom of God is not coming with things that can be observed, nor will they say, 'Look, here it is!' or 'There it is!' For, in fact, the kingdom of God is among you" (Luke 17:20–21).

This was not some political system that was going to be imposed by a divine ruler. Instead, as believers we must realize that when it comes to spreading news about the kingdom here on earth, it's up to us. What a tremendous insight! What an awe-inspiring truth! This idea was so radical that even Jesus's intimate followers did not grasp it. Jesus used many illustrations and made many projections, but much of his language was symbolic. The disciples remained confused, and this confusion still exists. The intense preoccupation with prophecies, second coming signs, premillennial symbols, and rapture expectations reflect this confusion. It's not surprising that marks of the beast, the four horsemen, and the opening of seals completely mystify sincere seekers.

Almost every culture imagines a future utopia, a golden tomorrow, a paradise of leisure and perfection, but some of these fantasies can stymy progress. It's easy for daydreams to replace dogged determination.

Jesus taught that the kingdom has more to do with practical efforts and productive lifestyles than with dramatic proclamations and wishful thinking. He indicated that it's in us or it's nowhere! It's now or it's never! It's real or it's all a cruel hoax!

Why would he have said, "The kingdom has suffered violence [from John's ministry until his imprisonment]," if it's a future event (see Matt 11:12)? Why would he have compared the kingdom of heaven to a tiny seed with tremendous growth potential if indeed it's something to be bestowed in the blink of an eye in a divine Parousia (see Matt 13:31–32)? Why would he have said, "The kingdom of heaven has come near," if it's really going to be established thousands of years from now (see Matt 10:7)? Why would he have said, "The kingdom of God is among you," if it's really something that is going to be installed by supernatural powers in the clouds of glory (see Luke 17:21)?

Much of the information about this kingdom is still in shadow. The geographical orientation, the cultural context, and the linguistic idioms make it difficult for modern men and women to understand. To first-century people who were immersed in royal realms, dictator states, monarchs, and rulers, the word *kingdom* had great meaning. The quality of their lives and the very continuity of their lives depended upon the conditions, privileges, and responsibilities of the kingdoms they occupied. It's hard for us to identify with their terminology because our world is different.

There is one thing we do know, however; this concept of the kingdom was extremely important! Jesus mentioned it over one hundred times. He proclaimed it, he described it, he compared it, he promised it, he prayed for it, and he longed for it.

Even though many aspects of this kingdom remain nebulous, some principles are clear. It's present, but it's not always accessible: "Jesus… said to his disciples, 'How hard it will be for those who have wealth to enter the kingdom of God!' And the disciples were perplexed at these words. But Jesus said to them again, 'Children, how hard it is to enter the kingdom of God!'" (Mark 10:23–24).

It's real, but it's not visible to everyone. Jesus said, "Very truly, I tell you, no one can see the kingdom of God without being born from above" (John 3:3).

Jesus explained its spiritual nature by saying, "My kingdom does not belong to this world. If my kingdom belonged to this world, my followers would be fighting to keep me from being handed over to the Jews. But as it is, my kingdom is not from here" (John 18:36).

It's inclusive but also restrictive. Jesus said, "I tell you, many will come from east and west and will take their places at the banquet with Abraham and Isaac and Jacob in the kingdom of heaven" (Matt 8:11). But he also said, "The gate is narrow and the road is hard that leads to life, and there are few who find it" (Matt 7:14).

It's obvious that the citizens of this kingdom will not be overly concerned about materialistic things. Jesus said, "It is the nations of the world that seek all these things, and your Father knows that you need them. Instead, seek his kingdom, and these things will be given to you as well" (Luke 12:30–31).

The benefits of the kingdom are valuable, but to enjoy them, believers must give up many things. Jesus said, "The kingdom of heaven is like treasure hidden in the field, which a man found and reburied; then in his joy he goes and sells all that he has and buys that field. Again, the kingdom of heaven is like a merchant in search of fine pearls; on finding one pearl of great value, he went and sold all that he had and bought it" (Matt 13:44–46).

What did this kingdom mean to Jesus? Why did it occupy his thoughts and monopolize his prayers? What is the significance of the kingdom of heaven? Obviously, it must relate to his other teachings. It must fit into and unify his overall message. It must synthesize his new commandments concerning life abundant, which includes freedom, forgiveness, love, and service.

Jesus began by declaring that, "Not everyone who says to me, 'Lord, Lord,' will enter the kingdom of heaven, but only the one who does the will of my Father in heaven" (Matt 7:21). Here he indicates that attitudes and deeds, not words and rituals, constitute the entrance requirements.

Jesus also said, "Unless your righteousness exceeds that of the scribes and Pharisees, you will never enter the kingdom of heaven" (Matt 5:20). Here he seems to equate the kingdom with morality and justice.

Many of his statements reveal he had great faith in the ability of righteousness and truth to eventually penetrate and change society.

He explained how "[the kingdom of God will continue to work in the world] like yeast that a woman took and mixed in with three measures of flour until all of it was leavened" (Luke 13:20–21).

Jesus admitted the kingdom had not reached a state of perfection at the present time. Not everyone accepted these principles of the kingdom. He said, "Again, the kingdom of heaven is like a net that was thrown into the sea and caught fish of every kind; when it was full, they drew it ashore, sat down, and put the good into baskets but threw out the bad" (Matt 13:47–48).

In another parable Jesus explained that both good and evil will operate together in the same realm over the short term. Yet he assures us that good will inevitably triumph over evil, saying, "The kingdom of heaven may be compared to someone who sowed good seed in his field, but while everybody was asleep an enemy came and sowed weeds among the wheat.... He said, 'Let both of them grow together until the harvest, and at harvest time I will tell the reapers, Collect the weeds first and bind them in bundles to be burned, but gather the wheat into my barn'" (Matt 13:24–30).

For this to happen, however, God's kingdom must reach every corner of the world. This will require the inhabitants of this kingdom to use all their abilities and skills in promoting its growth.

When a group of Pharisees and Sadducees came to John the Baptist, he said, "You brood of vipers! Who warned you to flee from the wrath to come?... Do not presume to say to yourselves, 'We have Abraham as our ancestor,' for I tell you, God is able from these stones to raise up children to Abraham. Even now the ax is lying at the root of the trees; therefore every tree that does not bear good fruit will be cut down and thrown into the fire" (Matt 3:7, 9–10). That was a harsh reprimand, but Jesus would agree! In a parable he said, "If a tree bears no fruit, it should be cut down. It's wasting the soil" (see Luke 13:7).

These passages indicate that individuals or religious groups who claim to be pious but do not reflect Jesus's attitudes and proclaim his teachings will be replaced. When we see the state of the world, it's evident many churches haven't "fed their sheep."

We live in a complex society with many problems and complications. Both educational and religious institutions have an obligation to prepare people to deal with a myriad of issues. It's not surprising that Jesus taught more than he did anything else. Men and women need to know how to think and how to discern facts from propaganda. They need to be able to separate truth from fiction. They need to be able to recognize con artists and dangerous demagogues. Jesus told us to be cautious about relationships, saying, "I am sending you out like sheep into the midst of wolves, so be wise as serpents and innocent as doves" (Matt 10:16). He constantly warned his disciples, saying, "Beware of false prophets, who come to you in sheep's clothing but inwardly are ravenous wolves" (Matt 7:15).

Churches must equip their members for service and then encourage them to serve. Too many have failed to offer aid and comfort to desperate people such as the homeless, the refugees, and others seeking sanctuary. Jesus was inclusive, saying, "People will come from east and west, from north and south, and take their places at the banquet in the kingdom of God" (Luke 13:29).

Churches have also failed to reach out with tolerance and compassion to those individuals who, because of handicaps, poverty, or different lifestyles, are yearning for understanding and respect. Jesus said, "Go out at once into the streets and lanes of the town and bring in the poor, the crippled, the blind, and the lame" (Luke 14:21).

Churches often fail to follow Jesus's example of expressing gentleness, kindness, and forgiveness in confrontational situations. Instead, they have allowed hostility and blame to cause divisiveness and conflict. Jesus said, "Be at peace with one another" (Mark 9:50).

Churches that strive for positions of authority and power and forget that their mission is to serve others will be replaced. Jesus said, "Some are last who will be first, and some are first who will be last" (Luke 13:30).

Self-righteous and critical congregations will be replaced. Those who follow the false words of evil men instead of the life-giving words of Jesus will certainly be replaced.

Churches should be finding answers to new questions and solutions to new problems, but most of them emphasize a few traditional doctrines over and over again, many of which are irrelevant in modern culture. Some churches tend to waste their credibility and resources by focusing on trivial matters and attacking minor flaws and faults. Jesus called this "straining out gnats and swallowing camels."

It's obvious that Jesus's gospel of acceptance and forgiveness is not the main theme of many churches today. Doctrinal disputes, morality codes, and judgmental attitudes are all too common among Christians. Even now, some important elements of the true gospel are being salvaged and promoted more effectively by secular groups than by religious groups. Sports, entertainment, and political organizations seem to show greater concern about prejudice and inequality than the local churches do. That has probably always been the case, because Jesus often enjoyed fellowship with "sinners" rather than "saints." He began his ministry in the synagogue but was rejected and threatened with death, so he taught at informal gatherings and even during meals with unbelievers.

God can still "raise up children to Abraham from stones." He can still use unlikely messengers to achieve his purposes. Therefore, if "orthodox" churches are judging and condemning or spending their time "swatting gnats" instead of offering the grace and love people desperately need, they will lose their influence and become obsolete. In fact, "The ax is already at the root of the trees."

Jesus gave a dramatic illustration about workers in the kingdom. He said,

> "It is as if a man, going on a journey, summoned his slaves and entrusted his property to them; to one he gave five talents, to another two, to another one, to each according to his ability. Then he went away. At once the one who had received the five talents went off and traded with them and made five more talents. In the same way, the one who had the two talents made two more talents. But the one who had received the one talent went off and dug a hole in the ground and hid his master's money. After a long time the master of those slaves came and settled accounts with them. Then the one who had received the five talents came forward, bringing five more talents, saying, 'Master, you handed over to me five talents; see, I have made five more talents.' His

master said to him, 'Well done, good and trustworthy slave; you have been trustworthy in a few things; I will put you in charge of many things; enter into the joy of your master.' And the one with the two talents also came forward, saying, 'Master, you handed over to me two talents; see, I have made two more talents.' His master said to him, 'Well done, good and trustworthy slave; you have been trustworthy in a few things; I will put you in charge of many things; enter into the joy of your master.' Then the one who had received the one talent also came forward, saying, 'Master, I knew that you were a harsh man, reaping where you did not sow and gathering where you did not scatter, so I was afraid, and I went and hid your talent in the ground. Here you have what is yours.' But his master replied, 'You wicked and lazy slave! You knew, did you, that I reap where I did not sow and gather where I did not scatter? Then you ought to have invested my money with the bankers, and on my return I would have received what was my own with interest. So take the talent from him, and give it to the one with the ten talents. For to all those who have, more will be given, and they will have an abundance, but from those who have nothing, even what they have will be taken away. As for this worthless slave, throw him into the outer darkness, where there will be weeping and gnashing of teeth.'" (Matt 25:14–30)

It's evident that Jesus pulled no punches as to how life operates! The principles of the kingdom are not sentimental and fanciful. They are not permissive and inconsistent. They make no exceptions for good intentions. In this parable, even the bystanders protested at the seeming ruthlessness of the master's evaluation: "He said to the bystanders, 'Take the pound from him and give it to the one who has the ten pounds.' (And they said to him, 'Lord, he has ten pounds!')" (Luke 19:24–25).

The surprising reply is adamant and unyielding. Jesus said, "I tell you, to all those who have, more will be given, but from those who have nothing, even what they have will be taken away" (Luke 19:26).

Jesus was not advocating selfishness or punishment. He was simply stating, "That's just the way it is! That's how things work!" As the old saying goes, "That's how the cookie crumbles." We may not like it, but we must admit that our own experiences and observations confirm this outcome. Those who have a lot of talents and resources do seem to get more while those who have the least often lose the little bit they do have. We, like the bystanders, may protest at the seeming injustice of such a system, but nature can't afford parasites! Workmen must be worthy of their hire. Each one of us must justify our space upon the earth because the kingdom depends upon it!

By analyzing Jesus's gospel, we've learned that his teachings dealt with the idea that we're to enter and help develop the kingdom of God here on earth rather than to eagerly wait for some future paradise. He was able to emphasize this revolutionary principle by separating truth from tradition.

Section 3

Purposes of the Gospel

Chapter 7

To Live It, Not Just Tell It

"I by my works will show you faith." (Jas 2:18)

In the Broadway show *My Fair Lady*, Eliza Doolittle confronts a would-be lover with a similar rebuff, saying, "Don't tell me. Show me!" When presented with the gospel, the world today wants actions, not words. Non-Christians are saying, "Don't criticize my life. Show me yours!" It doesn't help to say "God loves you" unless we are exemplifying that love.

When we examine Jesus's style and ministry, the first purpose we notice is that we're to show, not just tell, the gospel. People are influenced by deeds, not doctrines; by examples, not explanations; by demonstration, not debate. Skeptical individuals are looking for the real thing. They yearn for life with eternal dimensions. The preacher may preach it on Sunday, but the crux of the matter lies in how the members live it on Monday.

Jesus said, "You will be my witnesses" (Acts 1:8). He didn't say, "You *should* be my witnesses" or "You *ought* to be my witnesses" or even "You *must* be my witnesses." Instead, he said, "You *will* be my witnesses." For a believer, the question isn't "Am I going to be a witness?" That's settled. If you bear his name as a Christian, you are already a witness. The crucial question is "What kind of witness will you be?"

A witness is one who has experienced something personally and is willing to verify it. When a witness attests to an event, he makes the matter believable. A court is more concerned with what that witness is than with what he says. One word from a reliable person of good character carries more weight than a voluminous report from a shifty reprobate. There are many cases when "your actions speak so loudly, I can't hear a word you're saying."

Also, a witness has a limited role to play. He doesn't have to prove or argue; lawyers do that! He doesn't need to condemn or pronounce guilt; juries do that! He certainly isn't expected to hand down a sentence or punish; judges do that! The scriptures do not say, "You shall be my lawyers, my juries, or my judges."

Furthermore, the one who gives an acceptable report must be an eyewitness. No hearsay is permissible in court. Witnesses have only one obligation: They must relay honest information and give a complete report. But they have no responsibility as to the outcome. Of course, the more reliable the witnesses are, the better the case will be.

The same thing is true in the matter of spreading the gospel. Witnessing is what you are, what you say, and what you do, and these three must agree. Witnessing is being true to your own personal experiences. It's relating what you know in the depth of your being. A witness is false if it attempts to go beyond this point.

One of the rewards of being a witness is that we never know all the beneficial effects of our words and actions.

When Stephen was being stoned to death, he forgave his tormentors. His courage and faith influenced Paul. Then Paul influenced thousands. Andrew introduced his brother Peter to Jesus, and Peter became a church leader.

The Philippian jailer and all his family were baptized. The scriptures say, "Then he brought them outside and said, 'Sirs, what must I do to be saved?' They answered, 'Believe in the Lord Jesus, and you will be saved, you and your household.' They spoke the word of the Lord to him and to all who were in his house. At the same hour of the night he took them and washed their wounds; then he and his entire family were baptized without delay" (Acts 16:30–33).

The Samaritan woman influenced a whole city. The scripture says, "Many Samaritans from that city believed in him because of the woman's testimony" (John 4:39).

Concern for others motivates believers. They know it's a sin to hoard blessings, squelch insights, and hide truth. A man who has food and will not provide a portion to a starving brother is selfish. A person who is aware that a bomb is about to explode in a building and neglects to warn the occupants is irresponsible. A scientist who has a cure for cancer but withholds it from a dying child is cruel.

As Christians, we have blessings, insights, and truths that must be shared. Each Christian is commissioned to continue Jesus's ministry. This doesn't mean all of us must become priests or preachers. Doctors can heal in Jesus's name. Teachers can teach in Jesus's name. Farmers can feed the hungry in Jesus's name. Other believers can use their professions, their jobs, and their volunteer work to protect, support, and encourage those around them in Jesus's name. We have a responsibility to walk in the world for Christ. Jesus made that clear when he prayed this prayer: "As you have sent me into the world, so I have sent them into the world" (John 17:18).

Each one of us is expected to reflect our own particular facet of God's character. We're to be conduits of God's love to those who are hurting, just as a pipe lets water flow from the reservoir to the sink. We're to be conductors of God's grace to those who are in despair, just as a wire carries an electric current from the generator to the lamp. In short, we are to be spiritual liaisons between heaven and earth.

Jesus said, "Let your light shine before others, so that they may see your good works and give glory to your Father in heaven" (Matt 5:16). Letting our light shine includes the things we do as well as the words we speak. Our faith must have practical benefits and attract people by its consistency, sincerity, and truth. Above all we must avoid self-righteousness by admitting our own faults and weaknesses. Our flaws and failures don't disqualify us from sharing the gospel. Many Bible heroes were imperfect and still became successful witnesses.

God can use imperfect people. Noah was a drunkard (see Gen 9:20–21), yet "Noah found favor in the sight of the LORD" (Gen 6:8). Abraham was a liar (see Gen 12:10–13), yet Abraham was called "the friend of God" (Jas 2:23). Jacob was a deceiver (see Gen 27:22–24), yet he saw God "face to face" (Gen 32:30). Joseph was an egotist (see Gen 37:5–10), yet "the LORD was with him, and whatever he did, the LORD made it prosper" (Gen 39:23). David was an adulterer (see 2 Sam 11:2–4), yet God said, "I have found David…a man after my heart" (Acts 13:22). Paul was a persecutor (see Acts 8:3), yet he became Christianity's greatest missionary. Peter denied the Lord (see Matt 26:69–70), yet he was a leader in the early church (see Matt 16:18).

There are several personal qualifications, however, that Christians should exemplify. They must have respect and love. They must be compassionate and generous. They must be tolerant. They must have wisdom. These core values should be emphasized and practiced in every church.

Jesus was impartial and unbiased. He never labeled anyone by race, nationality, gender, age, or religion. He respected all differences. One group did not look religious. They didn't act religious. They didn't even know they were religious, but they ministered to hurting people. They fed them; they clothed them; they visited them when they were in prison and cared for them when they were sick. Jesus said, "Just as you did it to one the least of these brothers and sisters of mine, you did it to me" (Matt 25:40).

There is always someone watching us. They want to know if we practice what we profess. They especially watch our conduct during times of adversity. They note how we handle problems and face tragedy. Anyone can be happy and peaceful on sunny days, but it's what we do on stormy nights that indicates the depth of our Christian commitment. Sorrow, loss, and conflict are difficult for anyone to manage, but three things can help us overcome our troubles: First, don't personalize the issue. Remember that kingdom purposes are more important than personal feelings. Next, keep things in perspectives. Realize that current events and temporary problems may not be as catastrophic as they appear. Then, when you have done all you can do to alleviate your pain, just get up and go on. Don't dwell on the past.

When we interact with others, Paul told us to "encourage one another and build up each other" (1 Thess 5:11). He is right. Negative remarks and criticism can destroy our witnessing opportunities, but sometimes complaints and reprimands may be necessary. These suggestions will help: Stick to one problem at a time, and don't keep repeating. Always separate behavior from character. Individuals can't change their basic dispositions, but they can change their overt actions. Avoid sarcasm and ridicule.

It's obvious that many individuals do have antisocial behavior, and often Christians have to interact with these disagreeable people. When that happens, these suggestions will help us demonstrate a Christlike attitude: With defensive and touchy individuals, forgive and forget; don't try to make them feel guilty. With hostile and antagonistic individuals, accept them as they are; don't try to change them. With depressed and pessimistic individuals, approve and encourage them; quit condemning their attitudes. With complaining and miserable individuals, praise and appreciate them; quit taking them for granted. With anxious and unproductive individuals, recognize and support them; quit blaming and censoring them. Such aggravating people may be obnoxious because they need acceptance, approval, and appreciation, and they will remain that way until their needs are met.

To show our faith, we must use all our strengths and abilities. Every person has some potential area of strength. Some people are friendly and popular; they are good with public relations. Others are logical and productive; they get things done. Some are persistent and deep-minded; they can be good scientists or researchers. Others are tactful and diplomatic; they can be peacemakers and willing followers. It's important to find your specific abilities and use your skills.

Wise believers can take advantage of opportunities to share their faith. Once, a new handyman did a task for a single mom but refused payment. When she asked why, he replied, "Our preacher says we are saved to serve, so I always do one repair job free of charge. Then when they ask me why, I give them my Christian witness." People need to realize that witnessing is not dropping tracts from an airplane or displaying large "Jesus Saves" signs in your yard. We may know all the religious rules and look the way we think Christians should look, but if we disregard the day-to-day matters, God isn't fooled. We have to consistently "walk our talk."

Jesus recognized those who didn't. He said, "This people honors me with their lips, but their hearts are far from me" (Matt 15:8).

Being a Christian is a way of life. Many people see no connection between Sunday's sermons and Monday's activities. They talk a good religion, but they don't put it into practice.

When questioned about the gospel, Jesus said, "Love God; love people." This is the perfect definition of the Christian religion in four words. Each decision we make should be evaluated by that standard: If this word is loving, it must be said. If this word is not loving, it must not be said. If this action is loving, it must be done. If this action is not loving, it must not be done. This principle of love is more important than all the other doctrines and practices of our religious system.

Jesus cared about people. He never walked around pointing out defects in people, and he never tried to fix people. He even warned his disciples to avoid looking for flaws or trying to correct faults in others. Instead, he told them to solve their own problems, saying, "Why do you see the speck in your neighbor's eye but do not notice the log in your own eye? Or how can you say to your neighbor, 'Let me take the speck out of your eye,' while the log is in your own eye? You hypocrite, first take the log out of your own eye, and then you will see clearly to take the speck out of your neighbor's eye" (Matt 7:3–5).

In the story of the prodigal son, it's significant that the father didn't say, "Go take a bath, put on clean clothes, replace the money you've wasted, make a public confession of your foolish mistakes, and then I'll consider reinstating you in the family!" Yet, too often, that's the type of message we send to those outside the church.

Instead, the prodigal's father immediately hugged him just as he was in that dirty, disheveled condition. He put shoes, robes, and rings on him and affirmed his position of sonship before the prodigal had demonstrated any outward reformation.

It was John the Baptist, not Jesus, who asked for proof of conversion, saying, "Bear fruit worthy of repentance" (Matt 3:8).

Jesus knew things don't work that way. The priests and prophets had tried this method for thousands of years to no avail. Reformation can't precede grace! That's totally backward! It's the grace that enables the sinner to reform. Jesus said, "Those who are well have no need of a physician, but those who are sick. Go and learn what this means, 'I desire mercy, not sacrifice.' For I have not come to call the righteous but sinners" (Matt 9:12–13). Paul said, "While we still were sinners Christ died for us" (Rom 5:8).

We can't force, condemn, threaten or shame people into salvation. We can only extend God's grace and let it do its work!

We must respect people and regard them as our brothers and sisters. We must treat them as equals and remember God's spark of divinity is in them. Their social class or financial status is immaterial. We must show concern for both fellow Christians and those outside the fold. We are just as obligated to the unfortunate beggar in the slums as we are to the millionaire on Park Avenue. We should be just as respectful to the illiterate immigrant as we are to the intellectual physicist.

Our motto should be, "No man my slave! No man my master!" We're to love our neighbor as ourselves. Not as less, and thus despise him as an inferior. Not as more, and thus honor him as a superior. Mutual respect is the only relationship that will endure for the long term.

We must affirm people by always looking for the good and expecting the best. We must find the value and magnify the worth. We must ignore the negative and accentuate the positive. Jesus constantly said, "You can! You can! You can!": "Stretch out your hand" (Mark 3:5); "Rise up and walk" (Luke 5:23); "Nothing will be impossible for you" (Matt 17:20).

Jesus saw each person's potential and emphasized each person's possibilities! He described "such great faith" when he encountered the foreign centurion (see Matt 8:10). He called Simon "the rock" long before he seemed to be one (see Mark 3:16). He treated prostitutes, like Magdalene, as ladies (see Luke 8:1–2) and regarded deceitful men, like Zacchaeus, as gentlemen (see Luke 19:2–3). He did this because he knew the law of expectation.

The negative roles we assign to people often become their prison cells. We can't expect them to change if we as Christians are not willing to let them. On the other hand, if we assign positive roles to people, redemption and liberation become possible. People cannot be compelled to goodness. The law tried to do this for centuries and failed miserably. People cannot be persuaded to goodness. The prophets tried this, and although better than coercion, it still fell short. That's why Jesus's incarnation was necessary. Goodness can't be taught. Goodness can only be demonstrated and experienced.

We spread the gospel not by enacting laws, not by imposing rules, not by making speeches, and not by giving advice, but by living a godly life. We don't need more people who "believe in God." Instead, we desperately need more people who will live among their neighbors and reflect God. A spiritual nature is something that has to be passed from one living soul to another.

During World War II, Great Britain had little silver. They needed that precious metal to mint coins. After a thorough survey of the nation, it was discovered that some old churches had many silver statues of the apostles and early Christian leaders. In desperation the minister of finance made a decision. He said, "There's no alternative. Isolated, insulated, encapsulated saints sitting around in ivory towers are useless. We must melt them down and put them into circulation." That's exactly what the gospel tells us to do. People need to see our Christlike behavior much more than they need to hear our pious words! After all, "an ounce of example is worth a pound of advice!"

By analyzing Jesus's gospel, we've learned that we should show others the way by living it rather than by telling them about it. We can only achieve this purpose by separating truth from tradition.

Chapter 8

To Enrich Lives, Not Just Win Souls

"I came that they may have life and have it abundantly." (John 10:10)

Christianity is more than a heaven to gain; it's a life to live! The gospel calls people to wholeness of character.

When we examine Jesus's style and ministry, we discover that the second purpose of his gospel is to enrich lives, not just win souls.

When we study Jesus's life and activities, we don't find him going around repeating "the plan of salvation" to everyone he meets. When John the Baptist asked for information, Jesus described his ministry this way, saying, "Go and tell John what you hear and see: the blind receive their sight, the lame walk, those with a skin disease are cleansed, the deaf hear, the dead are raised, and the poor have good news brought to them" (Matt 11:4–5). He actually made people's lives better in many ways. He provided wine at a wedding; he held children on his lap; he relieved physical pain; he told stories about hidden treasures and lost sheep. He cautioned carpenters about counting the cost of construction and even gave good advice to fishermen.

Jesus used many models and figures of speech to describe the Christian's responsibility to others. He compared our spiritual influence to leaven, saying, "The kingdom of heaven is like yeast that a woman took and mixed in with three measures of flour until all of it was leavened" (Matt 13:33).

Leaven is silent and unseen. It works behind the scenes with no hope of personal glory. We don't expect people to say, "My, what marvelous yeast you used in this bread." Rather, we expect them to praise the end product—the bread itself—with no mention of the life-giving substance that made it possible.

Leaven must not be encapsulated. To work it has to interact with the other ingredients. It must permeate the lump of dough and give up its own personal identity.

For a loaf of bread to result, the yeast and the dough must be brought together. The rising occurs naturally when circumstances are right. Likewise, Christians must be willing to disregard their own egos. The purpose of the gospel involves bringing together the yeast of the spirit and the dough of the world. The rising is God's part.

Jesus also said, "You are the salt of the earth" (Matt 5:13). Salt, like yeast, must take a subordinate position. There are no compliments for the "yummy salt" in this soup or on this baked potato. Salt preserves, flavors, and enhances all food, but it has to mix with its surroundings to do any good.

Then Jesus said, "You are the light of the world" (Matt 5:14). Again, light isn't self-serving. A candle doesn't burn for itself, but for others. There is little notice taken of "that gorgeous light." Indeed, people are usually totally unaware of it when it's doing its job. They simply perform the normal activities that light makes possible. It's only when the light is not present and functioning that notice is taken and complaints are heard.

Spiritual light dispels ignorance, reveals falseness, and enables the kingdom to develop. To do this, the light must be on a candlestick, not under a bushel basket!

Light is positive. All the darkness in the world cannot put out one candle. Nevertheless, a candle without a flame can never light anything. That's why we're admonished to "let our light shine." Don't dim or diminish your light with apathy and inertia. Don't cover or hide your light with false humility. Don't discredit your gifts and talents by ignoring or denying them. If you have a special ability or an unusual interest and skill, use them!

Our calling as Christians is to a life of service, which includes extending forgiveness, healing wounds, and providing support. We shouldn't be overly concerned about getting credit for our accomplishments, because the pleasure of seeing the productive results of our efforts is its own reward.

Jesus often rejoiced over small successes. Once, after his encounter with the woman at the well, the scripture says, "The disciples were urging him, 'Rabbi, eat something.' But he said to them, 'I have food to eat that you do not know about.... My food is to do the will of him who sent me and to complete his work" (John 4:31–34). A Christian is a Christ-one, and Jesus himself said, "I came not to be served but to serve" (Matt 20:28).

Ministry is an important element of the gospel. Paul knew it takes time and patience. That's why he said, "Since it is by God's mercy that we are engaged in this ministry, we do not lose heart" (2 Cor 4:1).

Every Christian has something to contribute. The way a church or a community or a nation treats "the forgotten ones" and "the least of these" is a sign of God's presence or absence in that place.

The gospel commands us to provide nourishment. When Jesus told Simon Peter to "feed my sheep" (see John 21:15–17), he wasn't talking about casseroles or hamburgers or apple pie. He was emphasizing the importance of spiritual food. This food includes whatever is necessary to sustain and enhance life. Spiritual food is truth—as opposed to superstition, delusion, and perversion. It is righteousness—as opposed to injustice, partiality, and deceit. It is love—as opposed to hate, resentment, and envy.

Jesus met real physical, mental, and emotional needs with real physical, mental, and emotional food. He didn't give snakes, scorpions, and stones to a hungry world, and neither should we (see Luke 11:12).

There are a lot of medical facilities and mental health resources in our world today, but many problems remain. Homelessness, violence, abuse, divorce, and suicides are all common tragedies.

The psalmist said, "This is the day that the LORD has made; let us rejoice and be glad in it" (Ps 118:24). But most of us say, "I won't be happy today. I'll only be happy when I've got a better job, when I'm out of debt, when I get married, when I get divorced, when I have children, or when my children are grown." We all seem to think there's an ideal time and place out there somewhere, and if we can just find it, we'll be happy. But that's not true! Happiness doesn't depend upon entertaining events or perfect situations. Authentic lives and meaningful purposes make us happy.

No human being has everything his body requires or his mind desires. We all have unmet needs, frustrated desires, and unexpressed longings. We think we want more money, more pleasure, and more things, but what do we really want? We want to survive. We want someone to provide for us. We want to be protected. We want someone to take care of us. We say, "Please don't leave me; I want to be accepted." We say, "Please know me; I want to be understood." We say, "Please give me a purpose; I want to be useful." We say, "Please take my side in conflicts; I want to be supported." We say, "Please tell me I'm okay; I want to be approved." We say, "Please notice me; I want to be admired." We say, "Please be grateful for my contributions; I want to be appreciated." We say, "Please let me help you; I want to be needed." Above all, however, we want to be loved, but we don't say that!

Jesus knew that filling needs and healing pain were crucial parts of the gospel. He based his life and ministry on the scripture that said, "The Spirit of the Lord is upon me, because he has anointed me to bring good news to the poor. He has sent me to proclaim release to the captives and recovery of sight to the blind, to set free those who are oppressed, to proclaim the year of the Lord's favor" (Luke 4:18–19). Later, he sent his followers out to "cure the sick" (Luke 10:9). In his parable of the good Samaritan, Jesus complimented a man because he cared for an injured stranger.

Enabling people to enjoy wholeness and health is one of the greatest needs in our world today. There's so much pain and distress. From mass shootings to cruel bullying, from road-rage to domestic abuse, people are hurting. Many of these individuals can't attain true wholeness without physical, mental, and emotional therapy. That's why emergency rooms and surgical hospitals are not enough. Christianity stands or falls on its ability to heal and transform human nature.

Believers are expected to aid people who are in trouble. There are two Greek words for *burden* in the New Testament. One means something like a backpack. Paul said, "All must carry their own loads" (Gal 6:5). He meant there are some things other people can't do for us. We must learn how to do these things for ourselves.

There is a second word for burden, however, that means an overload. Paul gives different advice for these, saying, "Bear one another's burdens, and in this way you will fulfill the law of Christ" (Gal 6:2). This indicates there are loads too heavy for one person to carry. These come from such things as crises, accidents, misfortunes, and sorrows. Paul says we should help people bear such heavy burdens because these sufferers need more than our good wishes and sympathy. They need more than our thoughts and prayers. Christians should be willing to comfort and encourage their neighbors when they're experiencing grief, depression, and loneliness. Reaching out to the heavy-laden is a mark of true Christianity.

The gospel discourages idleness. Successful people plan while others sleep. They work while others play, and they do what needs to be done while others procrastinate. Jesus said, "Well done, good and trustworthy slave; you have been trustworthy in a few things; I will put you in charge of many things" (Matt 25:21). Paul said, "We work together with him" (2 Cor 6:1). You'll notice that in Jesus's parable about the goats and sheep at the judgment, he didn't say, "Blessed are you because you thought it" or "Blessed are you because you said it," but "Blessed are you because you did it" (see Matt 25:31–40). Work is sacred.

Christians also have a responsibility to warn others of danger. The scriptures say,

> "So you, mortal, I have made a sentinel for the house of Israel; whenever you hear a word from my mouth, you shall give them warning from me. If I say to the wicked, 'O wicked ones, you shall surely die,' and you do not speak to warn the wicked to turn from their ways, the wicked shall die in their iniquity, but their blood I will require at your hand. But if you warn the wicked to turn from their ways and they do not turn from their ways,

the wicked shall die in their iniquity, but you will have saved your life." (Ezek 33:7–9)

Sentinels have an obligation to observe the conditions around them and caution others of possible problems. The Old Testament prophets were sentinels, but many of them were persecuted and killed because they dared to express the truth. We desperately need some responsible modern-day sentinels. These must include excellent teachers and dedicated preachers, but they must also include an alert media with astute reporters, editors, and newscasters. There are several requirements that regulate a good sentinel's behavior: He must never desert his post. He must not become apathetic. He must accurately report pertinent information, but he must not squander his credibility by "crying wolf" just to get attention when there's no imminent threat.

Different people have different talents and callings. Paul said, "He himself granted that some are apostles, prophets, evangelists" (Eph 4:11). Evangelists don't have to be ordained professionals. An evangelist can be any believer who shares his faith.

Christians are under orders to express the gospel as they comprehend and experience it. The particular facet that each unique believer can communicate has never been heard before and will never be heard again.

Communication requires mental development and knowledge. Jesus taught more than he did anything else. His last advice to his followers was to "go therefore and make disciples of all nations" (Matt 28:19). Being a disciple means being a learner, and avid learners are rare. It's much harder to make disciples than it is to merely make converts.

Paul said, "What you have heard from me through many witnesses entrust to faithful people who will be able to teach others as well" (2 Tim 2:2).

The scripture even compares us to letters! Paul said, "You yourselves are our letter, written on our hearts, known and read by all, and you show that you are a letter of Christ, prepared by us, written not with ink but with the Spirit of the living God, not on tablets of stone but on tablets that are human hearts" (2 Cor 3:2–3).

If you're sincere, then the "gospel according to you" will always be a best-seller. The love of God is only influential when it is embodied in a believer! We are epistles or messages. We are living scripture to be read by a waiting world!

Christians are also ambassadors! Paul said, "We are ambassadors for Christ, since God is making his appeal through us; we entreat you on behalf of Christ: be reconciled to God" (2 Cor 5:20).

Diplomats and envoys speak and act for the party they represent, and we represent God! God reveals himself in nature, in Jesus, in the scriptures, in all people of good will, and in each of us. As his messengers we must be authentic and responsible. To reach a complex, diversified world, God needs numerous individual emissaries. There is not a preacher or an evangelist on earth who can do the task meant for you! There are people only you can reach! You may be your neighbor's messiah and his only link to spiritual possibilities.

Jesus called us fishermen. He said, "Follow me, and I will make you fishers of people" (Matt 4:19). Every Christian is commissioned to fish! When Jesus called Philip, he immediately began to search for Nathaniel. This response is natural for any person who has a real salvation experience. This desire to catch others is analogous to the attitude of avid anglers who are obsessed with obtaining their query.

Dedicated fishermen have certain common characteristics: They're patient; casting and trolling hour after hour without a nibble doesn't frustrate them. They're optimistic; tomorrow is always another day, and the big one is just around the bend. They're persistent. Once, Jesus told Peter to "put out into the deep water and let down your nets for a catch." And Peter answered and said, "Master, we have worked all night long but have caught nothing. Yet if you say so, I will let down the nets." When they did, they enclosed a great quantity of fish (see Luke 5:1–11).

Also, fishermen expect inconvenience, discomfort, and even danger as they seek out the best and most productive areas to fish. No serious fisherman ever drops his hook in the kitchen sink or a handy street puddle just because they are convenient. Remote and inaccessible places don't deter a true sportsman.

Fishermen know each fish requires a specific bait. What will attract one will alienate another. Therefore, he adapts his methods to each situation and becomes "all things to all people" that he may win some (see 1 Cor 9:20–22).

The scripture says, "The harvest is plentiful, but the laborers are few; therefore ask the Lord of the harvest to send out laborers into his harvest" (Luke 10:2). This doesn't necessarily mean we need more ordained pastors, evangelists, priests, or missionaries. Instead, we need more authentic, disciplined individuals who are committed to carrying out Jesus's mission.

Jesus often discussed sowers and reapers. Bearing fruit is an important aspect of the kingdom.

In farming, we're always just one season away from starvation. If we neglect our crops, we'll have no food. Likewise, Christianity is always one generation away from extinction. If the people of one era fail to pass on the torch, the next generation will be spiritually illiterate.

The purpose of the gospel is to save, improve, and enrich lives in a world that is full of broken ones.

To teach, counsel, or influence a person, we must speak their language. Jesus used simple stories and concrete, vivid examples. The scriptures says, "With many such parables he spoke the word to them as they were able to hear it; he did not speak to them except in parables" (Mark 4:33–34).

Those who help wounded people must be mature enough to put their own egos aside if necessary. Jesus warned about this, saying, "Can a blind person guide a blind person? Will not both fall into a pit?" (Luke 6:39). Peter added this advice: "Do not lord it over those in your charge, but be examples to the flock" (1 Pet 5:3).

Once, a minister was reciting Kipling's great poem. He said, "If you can keep your head when all others about you are losing theirs, if you can dream and not make dreams your master."

On and on he quoted the magnificent poem, always repeating, "If you can."

As the echo of the speaker's oratory rang through the auditorium, an old man with his face furrowed by tears stood up in the rear and cried out, "Oh, you are right, Sir! You are right! But what if we can't?" That's a good question. What if we can't? Or what if we don't?

As Christians, our responsibility is tremendous. Jesus said, "I will give you the keys of the kingdom of heaven, and whatever you bind on earth will be bound in heaven, and whatever you loose on earth will be loosed in heaven" (Matt 16:19). Yes, we have the key to abundant life, and we must share this treasure.

The early Christians didn't sit around and bemoan the terrible conditions of life; they changed them! The success of the gospel depends on the faithfulness of ordinary people. It's significant that only three of the twelve apostles are even mentioned in the book of Acts, while several laymen and women became essential ministers in the early church. Many ordinary Christians did great things: Dorcas sewed clothes for needy people; Cornelius gave alms generously to the poor; Ananias cared for Paul after his experience on the road to Damascus; Lydia, a businesswoman who sold expensive fabrics, opened her home to Paul and Silas. If all Christians would declare and express their faith in this manner, the world would again be "turned upside down" (see Acts 17:6).

By analyzing Jesus's gospel, we've learned that we should enrich lives rather than win souls. We can only achieve this purpose by separating truth from tradition.

Chapter 9

To Share with Everyone, Not Just a Few

"[God] desires everyone to be saved and to come to the knowledge of the truth." (1 Tim 2:4)

Jesus said, "You will be my witnesses in Jerusalem [which can represent our own household], in all Judea [which can represent our neighborhoods and communities] and Samaria [which can represent our associates and acquaintances], and even to the ends of the earth [which definitely includes every individual of every race of every nation in the world]" (see Acts 1:8).

When we examine Jesus's style and ministry, the third purpose we discover is that we should share our Christian experience with everyone, not with select individuals.

It's natural for people to be concerned about those they love. Therefore, most new believers immediately want to tell their family members what they have discovered. This was true of biblical characters: "Andrew…first found his brother Simon…and brought [him] to Jesus" (John 1:40–42).

The Philippian jailer was able to influence his entire household: "He and his entire household rejoiced that he had become a believer in God" (Acts 16:34).

Paul's concern extended to his national family, Israel: "Brothers and sisters, my heart's desire and prayer to God for them is that they may be saved" (Rom 10:1).

Even so, witnessing to their own family can present some of the greatest difficulties for Christians. This was certainly true of Jesus. His brothers and sisters were among the last to believe. They seemed to be resentful of his message and suspicious of his methods. They discouraged and rejected him, even to the point of doubting his mental competence.

Likewise, our well-meaning attempts to share Christ with our families are often misunderstood. Familiarity makes us less objective. Affection increases our emotional involvement, and conflicts may arise.

The first principle of any witnessing encounter is to allow the unbeliever to set the pace and lead the way. Most men and women don't really know their own innermost desires. They can't express their deepest feelings, and they won't admit their own inadequacies. That's why recognizing hidden needs often requires a sixth sense, which is God-given.

It's in family witnessing, more than any other, that a Christian's lifestyle has a greater influence than his words. Our parents, our children, our spouses, and our siblings know us too well to be fooled. They're aware of how we operate in every situation. They'll be observing us in greater depth than anyone else. This gives us an excellent opportunity to let "Christ live in us" daily.

Witnessing, in the final analysis, is simply spiritual counseling. Counselors must start where the person is and avoid all semblance of judgment. Good counseling includes both listening and advising, but the former should be maximized and the latter minimized.

Good counselors hear between the lines, then restate and clarify the individual's personal remarks. They never condemn, threaten, or display shock. It's especially important for those of us who are Christians to present ourselves as fellow sinners. Our transgressions may be of a different nature, but all of us certainly have flaws and failures. As recipients of God's grace, we can remove our masks and abolish our white-washed armor. If we're willing to share our own less-than-desirable attitudes and admit our own less-than-commendable actions, the hurting person will be able to identify with us and find hope.

Jesus expected his followers to spread the gospel and bring in the kingdom. Such outreach is inevitable and will continue if our spiritual experiences are real. That's because the moment the gospel becomes *my* gospel, I will have a desire to make it *our* gospel. Jesus described this mission message to the demoniac, saying, "Tell them how much the Lord has done for you and what mercy he has shown you" (Mark 5:19).

It may be hard to share personal feelings with loved ones or to relate intimate spiritual experiences to close acquaintances. Even Jesus had great difficulty with those in his own home and community. The devastating episode in the synagogue prompted him to quote the old adage, "Prophets are not without honor except in their own hometown and in their own house" (Matt 13:57).

Christians today can also be "without honor" among their old acquaintances and non-Christian friends. Quite often their first job is to change the negative impressions many people already have about Christianity.

Witnessing is not necessarily something you "go to do." Rather, it's something you "do as you go"! In the ordinary course of events, as you recognize needs, you should respond to them. Jesus seldom went to specific places to meet specific people. Instead, he found more than enough to do "on his way." We too can witness continually in our normal life activities.

As Christians we don't have to intrude or pressure people. If we're aware of spontaneous self-revelation on the part of others, we can respond naturally. Jesus witnessed on a well curb at noon; he witnessed in his room at midnight; he witnessed at festive parties; he even witnessed while he was dying on the cross. Our encounters will be equally varied if we remain spiritually alert.

There's an old story about a handsome prince who fell under a wicked spell. He took on the form of a frog and was told that the only way he could regain his royal potential was to be kissed by a princess.

This isn't just a fairy tale; it's a spiritual allegory. The world is full of people under a "frog spell." These nonproductive, unhappy creatures can only be transformed into sons and daughters of the king by a kiss. Christians have a divine commission to kiss frogs! Witnessing is kissing frogs! Ministry is kissing frogs! All around us there are frogs waiting and praying for the liberation that can only come when someone is willing to notice them, accept them, and affirm them.

Unfortunately, many church members are more interested in exterminating frogs than in kissing them, but someone must reach out because there is no other way that the frogs of this world can be redeemed. We must remember that under those cloaks of self-righteousness and beneath those hostile, defensive exteriors lies a precious, invaluable personality created in God's image. That person's potential can only be released when someone dares to offer love.

Jesus was the greatest "frog kisser" of all time! When he offered living water to the immoral woman at the well, he was kissing a frog. When he went home with the hated tax collector, Zacchaeus, he was kissing a frog. When he forgave the woman caught in the act of adultery, he was kissing a frog. Jesus always ministered to the neediest people. He helped the outcasts, the lost, and the "least of these." It's characteristic of Jesus that he never looked at what the person had been but always at what the person could be!

A believer's overflow of abundant life is what reaches out and influences others. When people look at us and say, "If your Jesus is like you, I want to know him," we are witnessing. Truly redeemed people don't have to "learn their lines" or "play the role of a Christian." They don't have to memorize a "plan of salvation." They don't have to be coached on how to tell others about Jesus. They don't have to be commanded to witness. Devoted fans never have to be trained how to support their favorite football team. Avid sports enthusiasts never have to be bribed or forced or commanded to boast about the athletes from their college. That would be ridiculous!

Likewise, if believers have a real spiritual experience, they won't have to be urged to share it. The woman at the well immediately returned to her village and proclaimed her discovery to everyone who would listen. She didn't attend any soul-winning classes or hand out any prepared literature. She simply told her own story. The "gospel according to me" is the only authentic gospel any person can share.

Responding to needs is a normal Christian characteristic. A soldier said, "A hero is one who, when he finds the way out of a danger zone, goes back in to lead the others out!" This is a vivid picture of witnessing.

Now, not every encounter will be successful, but failing isn't a sin. Jesus himself was disappointed many times. His hometown rejected him: "When they heard this, all in the synagogue were filled with rage. They got up, drove him out of the town, and led him to the brow of the hill on which their town was built, so that they might hurl him off the cliff" (Luke 4:28–29).

His closest friends and family misunderstood him: "When his family heard it, they went out to restrain him, for people were saying, 'He has gone out of his mind'" (Mark 3:21); "For not even his brothers believed in him" (John 7:5).

The rich young ruler walked away. When he asked Jesus what he must do to receive eternal life, Jesus said to him, "'If you wish to be perfect, go, sell your possessions, and give the money to the poor, and you will have treasure in heaven; then come, follow me.' When the young man heard this word, he went away grieving, for he had many possessions" (Matt 19:21–22).

Most of the population of Jerusalem was negative and hostile. Jesus said, "Jerusalem, Jerusalem, the city that kills the prophets and stones those who are sent to it! How often have I desired to gather your children together as a hen gathers her brood under her wings, and you were not willing!" (Luke 13:34).

Yet Jesus didn't let these unsuccessful experiences deter him from his mission. In fact, he told us exactly what to do when people reject us and we feel discouraged: "If anyone will not welcome you or listen to your words, shake off the dust from your feet as you leave that house or town" (Matt 10:14). This admonition means if we've done our best and failed to get a favorable response, we shouldn't second-guess ourselves or live with regret.

As far as we know, Jesus didn't go after the rich young ruler and beg him to reconsider. He didn't stay in Jerusalem and hold endless evangelistic crusades. Instead, in every case when his messages were not received, he went on to more hospitable areas. Multitudes of people today are silently pleading, "If you have life-giving leaven, share it with me. If you are the salt of the earth, let me taste your savor. If you are the light of the world, shine on me. If you have the water of life, give me something to drink. If you have the bread of heaven, give me something to eat." We must not ignore these unspoken pleas, because there's a world waiting for help.

If the whole world is our arena, then we will need maturity, depth of understanding, and great respect for personal differences. Global outreach requires many essential qualities. First, we must avoid intolerance. As we recognize that each person has a unique perspective on life, we must be willing to adapt and change our own opinions and expectations. We must allow people with other beliefs and lifestyles to have all the rights we have. For instance, if we insist on reading our Bible aloud in a public-school classroom, we must be willing to let Muslims read the Koran and other groups read their literature. Sometimes this is hard for Christians to understand, but we live in a democracy.

Jesus encouraged such diversity: "People will come from east and west, from north and south, and take their places at the banquet in the kingdom of God" (Luke 13:29). He didn't put people into categories. He complimented a Roman centurion. He praised several Samaritans. He admired the retort of a Greek woman. He defended female participation, and he gave special attention to little children. If we witness to "the ends of the earth," that includes a lot of races and nationalities.

On a bright night the two-hundred-inch telescope on Mt. Palomar in California can photograph stars one hundred million light years away. That point in space is the rim of the world for the astronomers who work there. If you draw a circle of concern that includes only you, your family, your neighbors, or your nation, then that's the rim of your world. But God's love encompasses the universe.

The personal commission of every believer is, "Come and see! Then go and tell!" Modern individuals want to see Christianity in action. Churches, congregations, and individuals must remove the enormous credibility gap that their unconcern and neglect have created. To propagate a great gospel, we must exemplify great lives. Taking the gospel to all the world isn't as hopeless a task as it might seem. The multiplying principle is tremendously effective. The good news could spread very quickly if every believer answered the call.

Once, a truck was involved in a traffic accident. The driver was pinned between the cab seat and the steering wheel. To make matters worse, the fuel tank was leaking gas, threatening an explosion.

Several motorists stopped and stood around, wondering what to do, when a man in a pickup jumped from his vehicle and ran to the wreck. He jerked the door open and crawled inside. He planted his feet firmly on the floor, positioned his shoulders on the crushed cab, and slowly straightened his body. This created just enough space for the unconscious driver to be removed.

When the rescue was completed, a policeman complimented the man who had rescued the victim. But then he asked, "Why didn't you wait for the emergency squad to arrive? They could have helped you." The man's answer was profound. "Mister," he said, "we always come to a time in life when things just can't wait, and this was one of them."

In the twenty-first century, Christianity has come upon one of those times. Our world needs the gospel with an urgency that just can't wait!

The task seems impossible, and success seems questionable, but we must try. There is one important scriptural passage that speaks to this issue: "Anyone, then, who knows the right thing to do and fails to do it commits sin" (Jas 4:17).

By analyzing Jesus's gospel, we've learned we should share the good news with everyone rather than just a few. We can only achieve this purpose by separating truth from tradition.

Conclusion

Jesus proclaimed an astonishing gospel! He accepted, forgave, and even praised sinners, but he criticized and castigated religious leaders. He said,

> "Woe to you, scribes and Pharisees, hypocrites! For you lock people out of the kingdom of heaven. For you do not go in yourselves, and when others are going in you stop them. Woe to you, scribes and Pharisees, hypocrites! For you cross sea and land to make a single convert, and you make the new convert twice as much a child of hell as yourselves. Woe to you, blind guides who say, 'Whoever swears by the sanctuary is bound by nothing, but whoever swears by the gold of the sanctuary is bound by the oath.' You blind fools! For which is greater, the gold or the sanctuary that has made the gold sacred? And you say, 'Whoever swears by the altar is bound by nothing, but whoever swears by the gift that is on the altar is bound by the oath.' How blind you are! For which is greater, the gift or the altar that makes the gift sacred? So whoever swears by the altar swears by it and by everything on it, and whoever swears by the sanctuary swears by it and by the one who dwells in it, and whoever swears by heaven swears by the throne of God and by the one who is seated upon it. Woe to you, scribes and Pharisees, hypocrites! For you tithe mint, dill, and cumin and have neglected the weightier matters of the law: justice and mercy and faith. It is these you ought to have practiced without neglecting the others.

> You blind guides! You strain out a gnat but swallow a camel! Woe to you, scribes and Pharisees, hypocrites! For you clean the outside of the cup and of the plate, but inside they are full of greed and self-indulgence. You blind Pharisee! First clean the inside of the cup and of the plate, so that the outside also may become clean. Woe to you, scribes and Pharisees, hypocrites! For you are like whitewashed tombs, which on the outside look beautiful but inside are full of the bones of the dead and of all kinds of uncleanness." (Matt 23:13–27)

He also said, "Woe also to you experts in the law! For you load people with burdens hard to bear, and you yourselves do not lift a finger to ease them" (Luke 11:46).

It's both disconcerting and disturbing to realize that Jesus's adversarial relationship was not with vile sinners; it was not with irresponsible drunkards; it was not with degraded prostitutes; it was not with hard-core atheists; it was not even with enemy soldiers. Instead, it was with orthodox priests, pious religious leaders, and authorized interpreters of scriptures.

They were Jesus's adversaries because they totally misunderstood the characteristics of the gospel. They misunderstood the concept that dealing with profound, not trivial, concerns is more productive. This is illustrated by the fact that they constantly dealt with petty, insignificant regulations and overlooked crucial issues like justice, forgiveness, and love. They "strained out gnats and swallowed camels" (see Matt 23:24).

They misunderstood the concept that using positive, not negative, approaches is more productive. This is illustrated by the fact that their complicated legal systems prohibited even the most humane and compassionate responses if these broke their Sabbath laws (see Luke 13:14–16).

They misunderstood the concept that presenting personalized, not standardized, requirements for salvation is more productive. This is illustrated by the fact that they made every convert repeat the same liturgies, follow the same rules, and perform the same rituals (see Acts 15:1).

These religious leaders were also Jesus's adversaries because they totally rejected the principles of the gospel. They repudiated the insight that God lives in men and women rather than in temples. This is illustrated by the fact that they saw no inconsistency in offering devout prayers to God in the morning and being cruel to their subordinates in the afternoon (see Mark 12:38–40).

They rejected the insight that power resides in truth rather than in traditional authority. This is illustrated by the fact that they believed counting out the exact legal tithe of dill seeds was more important than having virtues such as justice, righteousness, and mercy (see Matt 23:23). They also judged things by ancient taboos and traditions rather than by actual results and visible fruits.

They rejected the insight that the kingdom can be a spiritual reality that is among us now rather than a military or political realm to be established in the future. This is illustrated by the fact that they refused to embrace a rewarding, joyful lifestyle and, by the burden of their laws, made it impossible for other people to do so.

These legalists were Jesus's adversaries because they totally misunderstood the purposes of the gospel. They ignored the idea that we must show others our Christian behavior as well as tell them about our Christian doctrines. This is illustrated by the fact that they talked a pious script but lived lives that exemplified hypocrisy and cruelty (see Matt 23:29–36).

They ignored the idea that we must enrich lives as well as win souls. This is illustrated by the fact that their religious regulations and requirements were often legalistic and inhumane (see Matt 23:15–22).

They ignored the idea that we must share with everyone, not just a few. This is illustrated by the fact that they limited their outreach to one race, one nationality, and one social class (see John 8:33).

Their exclusive practices and narrow-minded prejudices made a mockery of God's love.

Now, if the gospel emphasizes these concepts, insights, and ideas, how should we minister? What did Jesus tell us to say and do? The common answer is to quote the great commission: "Go therefore and make disciples of all nations, baptizing them in the name of the Father and of the Son and of the Holy Spirit and teaching them to obey everything that I have commanded you. And remember, I am with you always, to the end of the age" (Matt 28:18–20).

These verses may define our ministry, but what do they really mean? They clearly indicate that we're to encourage men and women to be learners. It's significant that Jesus didn't say, "Make converts" or "Make believers." Instead, he says, "Make disciples." This term includes more than simply getting someone to agree with a doctrine. It means they must gain information, improve social skills, and develop personal discipline. We're also to immerse them in the deep spiritual concerns that characterize the divine nature of God. We're to teach them how to apply the moral precepts that will produce abundant life.

If Jesus paraphrased this passage, he might say, "Use my message to reach out and touch every human being of every race and every nation. Help them become serious spiritual students. Urge them to devote their lives to God's purposes, to obey and share my teachings, and to always follow the Holy Spirit's guidance. Assure them that if they exemplify attitudes and lifestyles that are compatible with my character and ministry, then I'll be present and active in everything they do!"

That's our commission and our promise. If we base our methods on those of Jesus and live out his values, others will see their merit and adopt them as their own. Jesus said, "God did not send the Son into the world to condemn the world but in order that the world might be saved through him" (John 3:17).

If God is in individuals, then we must respect them and treat them as if they were Christ himself. If we do this, we'll be obeying the command to worship God by serving others.

We must also discover information about the universe and adapt ourselves to reality. As Christians, we're expected to observe, listen, learn, and increase our knowledge in all areas of life. We have the responsibility as spiritual connectors to unify and synthesize such diverse subjects as science and theology, art and technology, politics and ethics.

Each one of us is an ambassador, an agent, and a representative of the divine realm. We must not merely "play God"; we must act for God by carrying on Jesus's ministry!

When Jesus said, "He who has seen me has seen the Father," he meant, "If you can't see God in the concern and love and service I exemplify, you will never see him!" Later, when he said, "As the Father has sent me, so I send you" (John 20:21), he meant that those who see Christians will see the Father. If the world can't see God in the concern, love, and service that each believer exemplifies, it will never see him.

Now, we're here on earth in Jesus's place. We're his understudies. John said, "As he is, so are we in this world" (1 John 4:17).

We are the only facsimile of God most people will ever be able to observe! God doesn't want us to make graven images of his physical likeness. Instead, he wants us to be living images of his spiritual likeness.

God doesn't love by remote control. He constantly involves himself in this world through those Christians who offer him their eyes, ears, hands, feet, and hearts. But problems arise and progress is slowed when our interpretation of the gospel is shallow, our performance of religious rituals is perfunctory, and tradition begins to supersede truth.

Once, a little boy had trouble keeping up with his friends because he was younger and smaller than the others. In group sports, people would laugh when they saw him trailing about twenty yards behind, yelling, "Come on, kids; follow me!"

Sometimes this seems to be the voice and position of the church. We talk as if we're leading the world when, in fact, we're trailing twenty centuries behind!

The gospel is good news, but it can be confrontational. Many people prefer illusions to truth. They reject any change in the doctrines and practices of their religion. Nevertheless, new discoveries and developments make change inevitable. The scripture says we "live by faith" (Heb 10:38). Faith is walking to the edge of all the light we can see and then taking one more step. This extra step requires courage, but it's essential.

The world, like Philip, is saying, "Show us the Father, and we will be satisfied" (John 14:8).

Each believer should be answering that plea by providing their own unique reflection of God, and that image must not be distorted. You can't see accurate reflections in funhouse mirrors. You can't see accurate reflections in muddy water. You can't see accurate reflections in dirty glasses. God is depending on us to reflect his character correctly and clearly. That's why the gospel we represent must be based on truth, not tradition!

www.ingramcontent.com/pod-product-compliance
Lightning Source LLC
Chambersburg PA
CBHW071008160426
43193CB00012B/1971